Beryl Mitchell, Scotland.

Jason Partner

With Pen and Brush

The Author demonstrating the art of water-colouring
(Photo Ron Bagley)

Jason Partner

With Pen and Brush

PROVIDENCE PRESS

TO AMANDA AND NICHOLAS

First Published 1987

Providence Press, Ely, Cambridgeshire

ISBN 0 903803 20 8

© Jason Partner

Illustrations originated by
East Anglian Engraving Limited, Norwich

Designed, typeset and printed by
Ashwell Print Services Ltd., Shotesham, Norwich

Contents

Acknowledgements

The author and publisher wish to thank Mr. & Mrs. J. Evans, Mr. & Mrs. P. Nevell, Mrs. J. Partner, Mr. & Mrs. N. Partner and Mr. & Mrs. J. Turner for permission to reproduce from original water-colours in their collections.

Acknowledgement is also made to Silver Studios, Godmanchester, for help in reproducing copies of old photographs and some of the water-colours, and to Eastern Counties Newspapers Group Ltd., for permission to use extracts from their newspapers.

Publisher's Preface

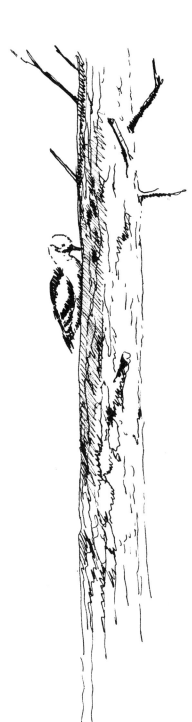

I first became acquainted with Jason's work when my attention was caught by one of his paintings which was being offered as first prize in a draw on a charity stall at Holkham Country Fair. It was immediately obvious that here was an artist who could depict the spirit of the countryside in the most delicate of water-colours.

In due course, my tickets were consigned to the waste paper basket but the painting had left such a lasting impression that I was determined to discover more about the artist. The opportunity arose early the following year when his annual exhibition was advertised in the *Eastern Daily Press.*

On the Saturday morning, the closing day of the exhibition, my wife and I visited the Assembly Rooms in Norwich to find an exhibition which exceeded my expectations – but all the paintings were marked with a red spot indicating that they had been sold. After a friendly chat with Jason, we realised that in order to purchase one of his paintings we should have to arrive on the first day of the exhibition, not the last.

Since then, I have had the privilege of joining the many clients who have become his personal friends, and it therefore gives my very great pleasure to publish his autobiography.

Those who know Jason will appreciate how fully he has taken on the 'cloak' bestowed on him by his respected tutor, Dan Watson. Dan's philosophy of life and his unassuming attitude to artistic ability has been remembered by Jason and absorbed into his own way of life.

Through the numerous talks and demonstrations which he has given to almost every conceivable type of organisation or club, he has broadened the artistic outlook of many people, including those who have wished to improve their own efforts, and those who do not paint but who have enjoyed seeing a true craftsman at work. His enthusiasm for his art, and his generosity and willingness to help anybody who has an interest in art is immense. His influence has spread far beyond the confines of Norfolk.

I hope this book will enable its readers to understand more about this talented and modest artist and how, through tuition, coupled with hard work, he has developed his natural talent to produce paintings which have not only brought him renown, but given great pleasure to many people.

JIM MASON

CHAPTER 1

Early Days

My grandmother Bott was one of four daughters of a well-to-do Leicestershire farming family. She was educated by tutors who went round the county instructing children in the normal school subjects and also in music, art, and in running the household. She could paint quite well and also played the piano. There is no doubt she was able to pass these skills down to my mother, who was an accomplished water colour painter, and also played the piano. Grandmother enjoyed a genteel life and never had to go out to work.

Sometime during Edwardian times the family lost much of its wealth, probably due to a depression in farming. Nevertheless I remember her as a very commanding person who was always dressed in a black brocaded blouse with a huge cameo brooch on the front near her neck, and a long flowing skirt, I never saw her without her black walking stick with its silver head. She lived in a large house and when I went there with my brothers and sisters if she caught us running she would say in a very severe manner 'Walk!' which had an immediate effect on us.

The only other grandparent that I remember was Grandfather Partner. He had a strong personality, gorgeous white sideburn whiskers and was very fond of fancy waistcoats which had become faded with age when I knew him.

'. . . an old bell on a metal spring clanged'

I was born in a little hamlet near Market Bosworth called Batram. It consisted of two rows of cottages beside a central road. Half way along, standing on a green was a huge oak tree with a seat round it. This was the focal point of the hamlet. There was one small shop in the front room of a house. Glass jars of sweets were always on show in the window, and in the background a wide assortment of other goods were on display.

When one went into the shop an old bell on a metal spring clanged, and there would be a few minutes to wait before the lady who kept the shop appeared from her living room. She was rather bonny and invariably wore a pinafore as was the common practice for housewives in those days. As a child I remember going in to buy sugared almonds which were about the size of a bantam's egg and came in many colours from white to blue and pink. These seemed to last for hours and I often arrived at school still sucking one.

The Village Shop

Various characters lived in the village and I particularly remember Mrs Springette. She was something of a wise woman to whom people turned when there was any sickness in the family. It was expensive to get the doctor and this dear lady was consulted first by many families. She was the village midwife and she brought me into the world. I was the sixth of seven children with four brothers and two sisters. My mother told me that when I was born Mrs Springette looked at me after a difficult birth and said 'What are you going to call this one?' My brothers and sisters had names popular then such as Arthur, Vera, Muriel, Harold, Alan and Walter. Before mother could reply she said 'You must call this one Jason' which was almost unheard of then. My mother said 'I can see that he has something in his hand like a pen and he will get his living by writing or using his hands and I will accept your suggestion and call him Jason'.

She also laid people out when they died. One of my earliest memories is of seeing the glass sided hearse drawn by a matching pair of black horses going down the village street.

Village events were held on the green. In the spring on Mayday the children danced round the Maypole with its gaily coloured ribbons. Round and round we danced until they were tightly wound round the pole. The boys then gave the girl who was nearest a kiss before we started off again until the ribbons were unwound. Then we were given sandwiches and home-made lemonade.

10

In the autumn everybody brought to the green anything which would burn to make a gigantic bonfire. There were not many fireworks because they were too expensive, but we had packets of sparklers, and the young children ran around waving their arms with them in their hands to make patterns of light as they moved about. It was a night to remember as we had potatoes roasted in the embers. When they were well done we split them open and put a piece of butter in. I vividly remember the feeling of being roasted by the fire on my front, while a chilly November wind sent shivers down my back as I stood spooning the delicious potato out of its skin.

The cottage where we lived was small with a front room, a living room and a kitchen at the back. Each of the cottages in the terrace opened out on to a yard at the back where there was a wash-house containing a copper and a sink. Whenever the latched door was opened there was a strong smell of soap. There was a deal table that had been scrubbed so much that the wood had been worn away and the harder grain of the timber stood out in fine ridges. This was where mother stood her wash basket.

The living room was a cosy place with a black-leaded fireplace which had hobs on each side. There was always a cheerful fire of wood and coal. The fireplace was protected from children falling on to it by a fender about three feet high with upright bars and a brass top and bottom rail. It was a weekly ritual on a Saturday morning for mother to get out the black-lead and brush it all over the metal work to keep it shining bright.

The mantelpiece had a green baize covering with a fringe of yellow baize. It was scalloped every 12 inches and had tassels hanging from each of the indentations. On the top were two well polished brass candle-sticks and a clock with a brown wooden face, which marked the passing hours with soft Westminster chimes. To one side was an old tea caddy with Japanese and Chinese scenes drawn in faded red on it. Where it had been handled frequently all the paint had been removed and only the bright metal remained. My parents used it for their savings which they used as a working float to pay odd bills as they arose. I never knew how much money there was in there, but I suspect only a few shilling although I remember it rattled as father or mother got it down.

The walls were papered, with a border along the top, and corner pieces of flowers, or fruit. The ceiling was lime-washed and was very uneven, in fact it seemed to bulge in some parts. From the centre hung a beautiful oil lamp, on brass chains. Above the glass chimney there was a metal shield but in spite of this the ceiling was stained by the fumes and the smoke.

Beneath the lamp was a table covered with a thick baize cloth which hung down nearly to the floor. I remember when we were young when we dropped anything how long this seemed to be, and how big the table legs were. If we were not very

The black-leaded fireplace in the living room

careful we would bump our heads on the side of the table when we were getting up. It was very solid and never moved.

On the floor we had lino which was used almost universally in those days. Mother bought this in a roll from a shop in Market Bosworth. It was father's job to put it down and he took great care to make sure that it fitted well, using an old pair of shears to cut it where necessary. But he had to allow for it to stretch and mother sometimes reprimanded him when he had not made enough allowance and it began to bulge. He would say that it would be all right in a few days time when it had settled. Then he would trim it down again round the edges.

12

In front of the fender was a home-made 'piece' rug. Making a rug was something in which the whole family could join. The children were given the task of cutting old cloths and rags into strips about four inches long and an inch wide. Mother bought a piece of hessian about four feet long and two feet wide into which she worked the cloth pieces with a hook made specially for the purpose. By selecting pieces of the same colour she managed to make some sort of pattern. She would mark on the hessian with a pencil or a crayon. There was an oval in the centre and in each corner a small circle. Probably the centre piece would be a band of red, with a ring of blue and perhaps another of white, and the colours were repeated in each corner. Most of the rug was grey as that was the most popular colour for clothing in those days. These rugs were terrible dust traps but they were warm and added a touch of luxury to our lives.

The chairs were all wooden and beautifully polished. One, which had belonged to my grandparents was larger than the others and was a honey colour where years of use had worn the wood to a glass-like smoothness. Then there was a rocking chair, with a tapestry seat and back. Mother was always worried that we would catch our fingers in this and tried to keep us away from it if anyone was sitting in it.

There was also a piano which was a magnificent piece of furniture made of dark polished wood. On the front was a decorated brass stand to hold the music and I have vivid memories of being there beside the piano and turning the pages as mother played. The top was permanently covered with a baize cloth to protect its highly polished surface. It had beautiful feet on its legs, and was very heavy and caused problems when it had to be moved when new lino was being laid.

Near the window on a small table was a pot with an olive oil plant with lovely glossy leaves. Heavy maroon curtains on a wooden rail with large rings hung at the window, and the door which opened into the kitchen, also had a similar curtain attached to it. This was to reduce the draught coming through from one room to another. The door was made of pine and had a dark varnish on it.

On one wall in the kitchen hung a small tin bath (the big tin bath was kept in the wash-house). There was a shallow sink made from a yellow stone, with a hand operated pump over it. The ceiling was liberally supplied with hooks on which hams and other meat could be hung. In the centre of the room was the usual pine table and chairs. All the household cutlery was kept in a drawer in the table. All the knives, forks, and spoons I remember seemed so big to my small boy's hands. Cooking pots and copper saucepans were ranged along shelves and the lids hung from nails in the wall. I was always conscious of how clean everything was kept.

Leading off from the kitchen was the pantry which was a world of its own because one entered through a latched door and down two steps into a room which was noticeably colder

The pantry

than anywhere else in the rest of the house. Along the white washed walls were raised tiled platforms called thralls which were used to stand things on such as butter, milk and meat, because these were the coldest parts of the pantry. A little light came through a tiny window set into the very thick wall. The walls were lined with well scrubbed plain wooden shelves on which mother kept her jars of pickles, jam, and all sorts of stores which she used for cooking. At one end father kept home made wines. There was also a range of large brown earthenware jars used for bread and bulky things.

Set into the floor at one end was a mysterious round stone with a metal ring which covered a well. Only on very rare occasions did father lift this lid, so that we could look down into it. It was a mystery to me as it was so dark when I looked in and I wondered how far down the water was. Sometimes father would allow me to drop a stone into it and count as it fell to get an idea of the depth. There was never any danger of falling in as the stone was far too heavy for the children to lift.

On another side of the room was a door leading straight on to the staircase. As on most of the doors in the house this had a latch instead of a knob. The stairs were made of polished board as there was no thought of carpet at that time. The small landing at the top led to a large front bedroom which my parents used, from which there was a perfume of lavender

14

which mother picked from the garden to decorate her dressing table. On one side was a washing stand with wooden legs and a marble top. A very large china bowl with a gigantic jug stood in the middle and on each side was a china dish, one for soap and the other for a flannel. A small towel hung on a rail on the side of the stand.

Under the window mother had a simple dressing table with two lace mats beside a mirror which was set into a wooden surround with a drawer at the base.

The bed was very large and I remember from the times when I slept in there for various reasons how soft the feather mattress seemed. It had a carved mahogany head-board, and was so high that when I was very small I had difficulty in climbing into it. There was a patchwork cover over the bed, which mother had made from fragments of material cut into squares and stitched together.

In one corner there was a wooden wardrobe with double doors and a carved corniche on top. This was where a straw case with straps was kept. All my parents' best clothes were hung inside and their hats were on a shelf above.

There was just one picture which depicted Christ knocking on a door saying 'Behold I am the light of the World'. Over the bed hung a text in a wooden frame which had crosses at the corners. It was printed on a paper which made it look as if it was embroidered. The words were from the scriptures and read 'I need you every hour'.

Across the landing were two more bedrooms where we children slept. Nowhere were the floors level and any furniture or beds had often to be wedged with a piece of wood or tile to make them stand properly. At night when we went to bed the linoleum floor was cold, but there was a rug on either side of the bed.

I shared a room with three of my brothers, but there were only two beds and two slept in each. Our clothes were kept in a chest of drawers made of pine with large white knobs.

Beyond the yard there was the garden with a path which led down to the hedge at the bottom and into fields. The path was made of cinders which came out of the copper and the fire, and was edged with bricks set at an angle so that there was a castlement effect. This fascinated me as did the mauve tinges of the cinders. I suppose that even them I was beginning to become conscious of colour.

Father's garden had rows upon rows of vegetables. He also grew the most wonderful gooseberries. When they were getting ripe towards the end of the summer he covered the bushes with old muslin curtains to keep the birds off. The gooseberries grew to a great size and I can remember seeing the faint bloom on them as I crawled under the branches to get the fruit without father knowing. There was a gorgeous moment when I had popped one in my mouth just before the skin broke and the juice flooded into my mouth.

'The privy had a tiled roof . . .'

Then there was rhubarb. Father sometimes gave us a stick which we took into the house where mother would give us a little sugar in a piece of tissue paper to dip it in as we ate it. There were also apple trees in every cottage garden and we had some to eat for most of the year. All the fruit was grown organically and free of any chemical spray.

In amongst the vegetables there were flowers, rows of sweet peas, poppies, or lupins. The men of the village took a great pride in their gardens and when they came home in the evening they spent most of the daylight hours working in them.

At the bottom of the garden there was the privy. This was brick built with a wooden door which sagged on its hinges and into which was cut a small diamond shaped hole to provide some ventilation. It had a red flagstone floor which was always visible as the door remained ajar when the privy was not in use. The scrubbed toilet seat had two openings a small one for the childen and a larger one for adults.

'He used an old brush . . .'

It had a tiled roof covered with ivy which I expect helped to keep the rain out. In spite of this I well remember sitting there and looking at the sky through the gaps in between the tiles. On the back of the door hung an old agricultural almanac, brown with age, advertising things like 'Wellington Boots 5 shillings', 'Buy your paraffin from Robert's', 'Morris Breeches from 7s 6d post free', 'Beaver Boots 19s 6d', and various other useful items which could be bought for a few pence. Hanging on a nail was a string with pieces of newspaper as in those days toilet rolls were a luxury that few people could afford.

When it was dark we used father's acetylene bicycle lamp, which was sprung so that when he went over a rough road the lamp tended to maintain its position and the light still shone on the road. It was operated by allowing water to drip on to crystals and took about 10 minutes to get started. This was the only light that we had until somebody bought one of us a battery torch as a Christmas present.

At night my sisters would ask for somebody to go with them as they said they were afraid of the dark. In the winter this would mean putting on an overcoat changing into outdoor shoes and then waiting in the cold at a discreet distance until they came out.

The walls were white washed and each year after a period of nagging from mother, father eventually got round to redecorating it. He used an old brush with the bent hairs, which hung permanently on a nail behind the door, to apply slaked lime which he mixed into a creamy paste in a bucket. I remember going in there when the walls were still damp and grey, but when they had dried out they looked snow white. He did not make a very fancy job of it but when he had finished he went to mother and said 'There you are Connie, fit for a duchess, fit for a duchess'.

Canada Geese over Blakeney Point

I never knew when mother learned to play the piano, but I can remember she also played the organ in the village church. She would often play hymns for us, and we would gather around and sing them with her. We had no inhibitions as we all joined in singing lustily and heartily. Father sat back in his chair smoking his pipe and although he did not join in he must have had a feeling of pride and contentment as he watched his wife surrounded by their children enjoying themselves.

On winter evenings we sat round the table playing, drawing, or writing and mother was always there encouraging us in whatever we were doing. I was mainly interested in drawing but the difficulty was to get paper. My parents could not afford to buy sketch books or pads or any other kind of paper. In fact they were not on sale in the village shop and were probably not very easy to obtain in Market Bosworth.

Mother saved every scrap of paper she could put her hands on. Envelopes were carefully cut up so that all clean unused pieces were saved. Neighbours were asked for any which they received and could be relied on to contribute generously. Consequently I learned to draw on pieces of paper of all shapes, sizes and colour. I drew on brown, blue, yellow and white. It was mainly pencil sketches as in those early days I did not have any paints as they were much too expensive to buy. I did however have some waxy crayons which could be bought in the village shop. These were kept in an old tin and even the smallest stubs were carefully preserved in case they could be used at some later date.

My sisters were very fond of doing jig-saw puzzles and spent hours and hours doing them. Sometimes I joined my brothers in playing with our lead farmyard toys. Father made us a plywood farmyard consisting of a house two or three barns and a path. After painting them he sprinkled sawdust over the red roofs, the path and the green fields to give them a textured finish. A piece of glass stuck on to the board was used for a pond.

The lead animals were set out in the field and we derived endless pleasure getting them out of the shoe box in which they were kept arranging them on the board and eventually at the end of the evening putting them away again. The box was lined with an old piece of velvet and each animal was wrapped to prevent the paint being scratched off. I started off with a few horses and cows, but gradually inherited all my older brothers' collections.

My set eventually included such things as round cornstacks, chickens, turkeys, small calves, a milkmaid with two tiny pails on a yoke, a fat farmer with his fawnish smock and red neckerchief, and a shepherd with a crook and collie dog. It was regarded as a great luxury to have some of the people with arms which moved. Then there were the farm wagons pulled by two horses and the really super ones pulled by four. We played at farms but this came quite naturally to us because we grew up in a county that was predominately agricultural. So we were really playing at the life which was around us. I loved my farmyard animals and still have some of them in my studio.

Mother had a Singer sewing machine which was more or less in constant use, either for mending or altering clothes which one of us had grown out of, to fit a younger member of the family or making something for one of my sisters. We waited eagerly for a cotton reel to be emptied so that father could make yet another tank for us to play with.

The reels were made of wood in those days enabling father to cut tiny notches in the rims. This he did with his razor sharp pocket, or shut knife. Next he got a candle (we had no electricity and used candles when we went upstairs to bed), and cut off a thin slice like a washer of wax about a quarter of an inch thick, from which he pulled the string wick to create a hole in the middle. Then he took four tin tacks, normally used for repairing shoes, and knocked two in on each side of the central hole at one end of the reel.

Now an elastic band was threaded through the reel, over the tacks at one end, and through the washer and over a match stick at the other. The match stick was then turned round to create tension in the band. When the reel was put on the floor the band unwound and propelled it forwards. The art was to wind the elastic band up as tightly as possible, but taking good care not to overwind and break it, as it was probably the only one we had and not easy to replace. We often played on the hearth rug which we moved around to create ridges for the

19

tank to climb over. A good tank made in this way would sometimes travel across the room before it unwound. We got endless fun from this simple homemade toy by making all sorts of obstacles for it to cross.

While we amused ourselves mother was probably knitting and father glancing through the local paper. He was not a great reader and seldom read a book. On the other hand mother enjoyed reading and encouraged us to do so as she did with her music and painting. Father was much more practical with ability to make things. Whenever anything was needed he made it if at all possible. There was insufficient money to go to the hardware shop and buy anything which could be made at home.

His knife was a well used tool whether it was cutting leather to make a hinge for a rabbit's hutch or to carve the head of a stick cut from a hedge. He would sit in the evening carving with a newspaper on the floor between his feet to catch the wood shavings. He had some lovely sticks with a variety of different well carved heads.

We lived quite close to the mining district of Leicestershire and Nottinghamshire. Out of sheer desperation for work at one time father was a miner. The idea of going down a shaft into a hole in the ground to get coal filled us with foreboding and I know my mother was very worried whenever he was at work. One day when he was stripped to the waist, working on a very narrow seam, some of the short 18 inch props gave way and father became trapped. His fellow workers managed to pull him free, but for a long time afterwards his back showed the coal dust filled scratches. He never went down the mine again because mother was so distressed by the accident.

Old cattle bridge on meadows near Aylestone

CHAPTER 2

School Days

Batram was in the heart of rural Leicestershire and was a few miles from the school which my brothers, sisters and I attended. All the boys wore grey clothes, grey flannel shirt, grey socks, usually falling around their ankles, and grey short trousers held up with a fabric coloured-banded belt fastened with a metal clasp in the shape of a snake. Each morning we set off to walk to school mother gave us each a packet of sandwiches as there was no such thing as school dinners. More often than not she used cold toast which sounds very unappetising but in fact was quite enjoyable for hungry children.

Our path took us over fields and as we walked along we were all the time observing nature, the changing seasons, and farmers working in their fields. We got to know each stile, each tree, each pond and yet the countryside was almost taken for granted. This was our entire world and we knew no other.

We had our favourite pond where in the spring we stopped to look for frog's spawn and as the season progressed we saw the tadpoles which eventually turned into tiny frogs. There were lovely parts where we could lie on the bank about three feet above the river and look down into the crystal clear water and see the teeming insect and fish life. There we saw caddis fly larvae crawling around in their self made 'houses' of bits and pieces gathered from the river bed. We saw minnows in their hundreds swimming about and gudgeon lying as still as stones amongst the gravel.

There was the old willow in a branch of which a mallard had its nest. It had partially fallen into the river enabling us to climb up its sloping trunk and look into the nest, in spite of it being well out into the river. We found birds' nests of many different species, by looking up through the hedges or searching in the grassy banks. We learnt to recognise birds by the way they moved, by their song, or by their flight, a flash of blue darting along the river was instantly identified as a kingfisher. We knew that a thrush hopped along and that a blackbird walked.

But however anxious we were to explore the hedges and meadows we knew we must not be late for school. When the teacher came out to ring the hand bell we had to be there as no mercy was shown to any late comers. The school was quite small and had a tarmac play-ground surrounded by an iron rail fence. I remember well the heavy metal cup attached by a thick chain to the tap. We somehow had a sense of hygiene and did not use it. Instead we put our mouths under the tap and drank directly from the flowing water. This was our only source of drink, winter and summer and we never had anything hot until we got home again.

Inside, the cloakroom was decorated brown up to head height and above that it was cream. There were big varnished racks for us to hang our clothes on, and often by the time we arrived our coats were very wet, especially in the winter.

Although our shoes were frequently wet from walking through the damp grass we had to sit in them all day as we had nothing else to wear. When we went home again after school our coats would feel damp and cold when we put them on as they had not dried out during the day. At lunch time brothers and sisters met together and we then ate our sandwiches providing we still had some left. Too often as we walked to school we nibbled our lunches until by the time we arrived there were none left. I can remember putting my hand in my pocket to break off a corner of a sandwhich intendng that to be the only piece, but could not resist another and so it went on until it was all finished.

Drinking cup at the village school

We learned to swim in the porridge pot

On the way home in the summer time as we walked along the bank of the River Soar the water looked so cool and tempting for a swim. At one point a place had been dug out so that cattle could drink. The current swirled round in this area which we referred to as the porridge pot and it was here that we all learned to swim.

On lovely hot days we stopped there and sooner or later someone would suggest that we should have swim. My sisters went in first and as we did not have any costumes they went behind the bushes and took their clothes off and slipped into the water wearing knickers and vests. Then it was our turn to go behind the bushes and when we had stripped down to our pants we called 'Ready, ready', which was the signal for them to look away as we dashed in.

A real problem arose when we got out as of course we had nothing to dry ourselves on. We did the best we could by running around and rubbing our bodies with dry grass, but our under-clothes were too wet to wear. Our best efforts at wringing the water out, or banging them against a tree were of no avail and we had to go sheepisly home knowing full well that mother would know what we had been doing.

One day on the way home my brothers decided to try to get some water-hen's eggs from a nest on a willow branch that was hanging over the river. Since I was the smallest, I was given the task of crawling along the branch to get them. Unfortunately we had not realised that my weight would depress the branch

'. . . my weight would depress the branch'

23

further into the water. Eventually my brothers noticed the nest gradually sinking into the water which soon began to flow in, causing the eggs to begin to float away. 'Quick! quick!, grab the eggs', one of them called, but I only managed to catch one. The branch by this time was swaying up and down and I could not get back still holding it.

'What shall I do with it?' I called.

'Put it in your mouth' came the reply.

I did as I was told, and then tried to crawl back up the branch, but this was much more difficult than going down it. Inevitable I lost my balance and plunged into the muddy water breaking the egg in my mouth at the same time. Although the water was not very deep I got thoroughly soaked and muddy. Harold took my clothes and washed them in some clean water in another part of the river, while the others rubbed me down with dry grass.

When we got home we implied that I had fallen in. We dare not mention that we had been trying to get eggs as father did not approve of taking birds' eggs.

Every year some of the meadows were cut for hay and the smell of it still brings back memories of these happy carefree days. Horses with jingling harness pulled great lumbering carts across the fields and the carters' voices calling 'Come on', or 'Whoa' carried over the quiet countryside.

Sometimes we made boats from a reed leaf, using a thorn twig as a mast and a dock leaf for the sail. Endless fun could be had by racing them down the river hoping they did not get entangled in overhanging branches on their way. If they did then we had more fun as we endeavoured to free them. Good boats lasted until we had to leave the river bank and make for home. On the way we crossed some lovely little bridges over the ditches in the meadows. I often wondered who took so much trouble to build them. They fascinated me and as I got older I often went back to draw and paint them.

On the river there were some grand old willows. From a distance the trunks were too shrouded in branches and leaves to be visible but nearby they could be seen to lean at all angles. On the river side often the bank had been eroded exposing the roots and causing the trunk to lean over the river. Then there were the trees where animals sheltered from the sun and flies and rubbed themselves against the trunks which were polished smooth. On one there was an inch thick rope with a knot at the bottom. Each took a turn at hanging on to it while one of the others pushed it out over the water. At the end of the swing you were well out over the river and I can remember hoping against hope that I would not fall in when it was my turn.

I remember best arriving home in the autumn when the colder weather was just beginning and being greeted by a cheery fire in the grate. We used to sit in front of it and make toast. When it was done mother used to spread it liberally with butter. Even better were the days when we had dripping from a

(1) Reeds grew in the river

(2) Reed wound from the centre

(3) Thorn inserted to hold reed together

(4) Sailing down the river

joint of beef or pork to put on it. As we were toasting we looked into the fire to see if we could recognise any shapes in the cinders. Sometimes we thought we could see a man's face, sometimes a bear, or a cat, or a dog. It all seemed fun to us and I suppose it helped us to develop our imagination.

Considerable skill was needed to get the toast well done on both sides. In the process your hand became very hot and it was necessary to change hands from time to time. There was also the problem of keeping a bed of glowing embers for the long period it took to make enough toast for a large family. After the toast with butter or dripping running down our cheeks there was a hot cup of tea followed by a delicious slice of mother's home-made cake. As a special treat we had butter spread over the cake.

Mother like most housewives at the time seemed always to be cooking. I took little notice of what she was doing, until the time came to make Christmas puddings. We all stood round the huge bowl in which all the sweet smelling ingredients were mixed and for good luck we all had a stir and a wish as we did it. Out of the mixture she made a number of puddings which were wrapped in clean pieces of linen which were saved for the purpose from any suitable discarded items of bed linen. The day that they were cooked in the copper the whole house was filled with an unusual but lovely aroma.

Sunday was a special day and quite different from any other. We wore our Sunday suits and our sisters put on their best dresses. Our shoes were always polished on Saturday evenings even if they were neglected for the rest of the week. We were not allowed to play in any way that might dirty our clothes and therefore spent much of the day playing indoors with our toys.

When the weather was good in the spring and summer, the whole family went for a walk to visit relatives or round the country lanes. The children all walked a little way ahead of the parents. I expect this was to make sure that we did not misbehave. As we went along father would make comments on the gardens we passed, perhaps praising some of the vegetables and flowers or perhaps saying that they did not look very good. He drew our attention to the crops in the fields, to the stacks and the way they had been thatched, and in fact to anything which he thought would be of interest. He looked into hedges where he hoped to find a branch or a young tree which might one day make a good walking stick. When there were wild flowers mother gathered some to take home telling us the names of each one as she picked it. Sometimes she found some herbs which she bunched up to hang from the kitchen ceiling to be used later for cooking or medicine.

In addition to mother's herbal remedies father had great faith in the curative value of honey. He often reminded us that the Romans spread it on their battle wounds because of its antiseptic properties. Many a time I saw him use honey on cuts and bruises he or we had suffered. Father usually took a jar of

Cattle in the meadows

honey in his food bag. At meal time I saw him pour it into his mouth straight from the jar. During our walks he made sure that we noticed the bees with their pollen sacks loaded, working on the hedgerow flowers.

Our family always kept at least one dog and from time to time each of the children had one of their own. I think one of the most satisfying and fullfilling things in a boy's life is to have the companionship of a dog. Jess was a black and white border collie cross sheep dog with a sensitive face and very intelligent. Whenever I went for a walk she was with me. She was easy to control as her inherent instinct was to be obedient especially if there were animals in the field. I knew that she must not chase them and she hardly needed to be reminded after she had been trained to keep to heel. In fields where there were no animals she hunted the grass and along the river banks. When I sat down to rest she collapsed beside me panting away with her tongue hanging out. Sometimes when I reclined I used her body to rest my head on as if it were a pillow.

We never went away on holiday. Summer holidays we spent in the fields helping with haymaking and corn harvest. The boys led the horses from one cob of hay to the next as they were loaded on to carts. Even as a small boy I remember looking up into the soft placid face of a horse and into its nostrils and tender muzzle. The faint purplish tint as it came down from the brown of the forehead and the wrinkles round its mouth where the bit was held in place fascinated me. When it rolled its lips up its grass stained teeth were exposed. There was such strength in those animals and yet they were so gentle. We had to be careful not to stand too close in case they moved and put a hoof on one of our feet.

At the end of the day the horses were taken out of the carts and if I was lucky I was allowed to ride one back to the farm. The route took us through a ford in the River Soar, and there we stopped while the horses had some drink. I had to unfasten the bearing rein to let the horse get its head down. Looking down its coarse hairy mane always frightened me and it was always a relief when it lifted its head up again and I could refasten the rein. At first the hooves left wet prints on the road but these soon faded in the dust. Then there was the steady clip clop, and jingle of harness as we slowly made our way to the farm.

My sisters often took the harvesters' food out into the fields in a large basket covered with a check tea cloth. Under it was a bowl containing a steamed spotted dick pudding with cold custard over it. There was also some cold tea in a brown beer bottle with a screw top, a knife and fork and some bread and cheese. While they ate the workers sat leaning against a hay cob or stook of corn.

Sometimes I helped to take the food and on occasions I sat with the men as they ate what we would call a ploughman's lunch. I particularly remember Alf who was then in his late sixties. He wore brownish trousers with thin leather straps just below his knees, which he said helped his 'Rheumatics'. Winter and summer he wore a waistcoat, his only concession to the seasons was to unbutton it if the weather was very hot. Under it he had a 'Melton' shirt made of thick material with red and purplish stripes. He never wore a collar but a shiny brass stud kept the band fastened.

During the summer he had a dark tan against which his bushy white eyebrows stood out in sharp contrast. His hat was an old battered grey trilby stained with sweat and water round its band. On the rare occasions that he took it off as for instance in the church where he was a sidesman, there was a very distinct line of demarkation between his tanned face and his white forehead.

He had a wonderful humourous way of entertaining boys as he ate his food. His favourite joke was to pretend that he had cut off his thumb while using his 'shut' knife to cut his cheese and onions. This knife had a curved blade and he would hold a piece of cheese or onion in his left hand using his thumb to hold it firmly to cut against. When he was sure he had our attention he suddenly dropped his thumb and tucked it into the palm of his hand. Then he would say 'Cor blast I've cut my thumb off, tha's somewhere down here can you find it Bor?'. We then all pretended to look for it, and when we were not looking at him he would say 'I've found it'. Then he popped it up again. We marvelled at what had happened the first few times but we soon learned how he did it, but this did not deter him from doing it again and again.

He had a great way with horses and could do anything he wished with them. To calm a horse he talked to it gently while he breathed into its nostrils. He knew so much about the countryside and shared his knowledge with us. He showed us how to recognise where foxes or hares were running, how a rabbit jumps and just the spot to set a snare to catch it.

'You won't need your coat today boy' he would say after glancing up to the sky. Over the years he had learnt to read the sky to forecast the weather which played such an important part in his life. You could rely on him as he was seldom wrong. He used to say 'I may be short in book learning but I'm long in life'.

One day I was with Alf carting pigs' muck away from the yard. I was quite small and he perched me on the front of the tumbril. The muck smelt rather high and was more fluid than usual. We came to a gate and Dolly stopped to Alf's command of 'Whoa'. While he went forward to open it the mare spotted a rat which frightened her. She reared up tipping the cart high enough to make me fall backwards into the muck. When I picked myself up I had the evil smelling stuff all over my back much to Alf's amusement. He grabbed handfuls of grass and wiped me down as best he could. After emptying the cart he took me home. Mother took one look at me got the bath off its hook and peeled my clothes off. She was very cross with Alf but he really took no notice and merely said in a rather casual way 'Oh that won't hurt him its only a little muck.'

Alf took and interest in our early courtships. I have heard him say to my brothers 'Which girl are your courting now'. The reply might be Peggy Brown and his comment 'Oh she's a lovely girl and to emphasise it, he like many a countryman, repeated what he had just said 'She's a lovely girl'.

Muck carting in Norfolk

One vivid memory I have of Alf was at a Harvest Festival in our local church. This was always a happy time of the year with mother baking loaves of bread in the shape of a sheaf of corn and father gathering flowers and vegetables from the garden. The beautifuly decorated church gave the service a very special meaning to the congregation who joined heartily in singing favourite hymns such as 'All is safely gathered in', and 'We plough the fields and scatter the good seed on the land'.

On the particular occasion I was pushed into the pew first as I was the youngest at the time. I found myself next to a window with it's wide stone sill covered with shiny red apples. Although we had plenty in our garden I decided to try to steal one. Holding my prayer book in my left hand I gently pushed my right hand behind my back up towards the apples. All was going well. I had actually got my fingers on one when I happened to see Alf looking and scowling at me. There was no need for him to say anything, his disapproving shake of his head was sufficient for me to immediately drop the idea of getting an apple. For the rest of the service I dare not look at Alf as I felt so guilty. When we left the church I hoped and prayed that he would not tell my parents but he was a dear man and said nothing.

As I grew up and spent more time sketching I often saw Alf in the fields. In those days I would draw an old tree, or a gate, or a post polished smooth where animals had rubbed against it, or a barn, or in fact any object which caught my eye. If he came anywhere near he walked over to look at what I was doing. After peering over my shoulder for a while he would mutter to himself, 'Well tha's a rum un aint it, tha's a rum un tha ole gate'. He always seemed slightly amazed that I had made a sketch of such an ordinary subject which through my work he could see in a different way.

Alf lived in a beautiful little cottage with a colourful flower garden in front and a neat vegetable patch behind. He was over eighty when he died and was buried in the churchyard close to the wall which separated it from the fields. I like to think that was where he wanted to be, close to the fields and cattle which had been such a large part of his life.

When I was about twelve years old the economic situation forced my parents to move to Aylestone on the outskirts of Leicester. Although we were now living close to a town we still enjoyed a country style of life. The village had its farms and a green where we played with our new friends. It was close to the River Soar, so we could wander through meadows along the river and Grand Union Canal which joined the river just outside the village.

The canal was very busy in those days and frequently a gaily painted horse drawn barge made its slow way along from one lock to another. At each lock there were rollers over which small boats could be dragged. My brothers and I spent many hours watching barges go through the lock and helping punts

Aylestone lock

and rowing boats over the rollers. Considerable use was made of the river for recreation, and at weekends and public holidays we earned pocket money in this way.

All the locks had a keeper who took pride in keeping everything in a good state of repair and decoration. A particular effort was made to have colourful flower beds wherever there was sufficient space. There was always great excitement when a lock was being cleaned. After a barge used for this purpose had been put into the lock, both gates were closed and the water gradually pumped out. As the barge went down the walls were scraped and cleaned. When most of the water had gone there were usually some fish trapped in the muddy pools which remained, these were netted and returned to the river.

Once a cow got into the canal and was drowned. All the children of the village ran down to see it hauled out as soon as word got around. On another occasion a person was drowned and the body pulled out on to the towpath. I happened to pass by and saw where it was lying under the local policeman's cloak.

The move to Aylestone was later to make my attendance at Art College much easier than if we had still been living in Batram.

The onion-topped mill near Barnack

CHAPTER 3

Art School

At the age of eleven I took the exam for entrance to Market Bosworth Grammar School and although I was never very good at the academic side I passed. I expect that even at this early stage my drawing helped me to be successful. A few years later I entered an art competition and was awarded first prize in the county of Leicestershire. The hours that I had spent sketching in the fields and the encouragement of my mother in my love of drawing had thus borne fruit. The prize consisted of a package of art materials, pencils, paints, brushes, and paper, so for the first time in my life I was able to enjoy using the best equipment then available.

Another part of the prize was to attend evening classes at the Leicester College of Art. There I met Mr Daniel Watson who as principal of the College had been one of the judges. This began a chapter in my life that was to have a profound effect on my career and future. It started a life long friendship with Dan who was later to become my tutor.

Dan was a strange man, in his dapper dress he looked more like a bank manager than an art master. He had silvery grey hair, wore a shirt with a winged collar and a dark blue cravat with a jewelled tie pin in it, a waistcoat, and striped trousers.

Dan Watson

Pop Atkins

He had a very quiet manner and made a lasting impression on me from the first time that I met him after winning the prize.

When I left Grammar School I was extremely fortunate to be able to attend the Art College as a full time student. At the time I was really too young but Dan managed to persuade the Governors, and the Education Committee that I was showing promise as an artist and that I would benefit from the classes.

After a few terms I gradually came more under the direct influence of Dan who was a brilliant water-colour artist, a founder member of the Leicester Society of Arts and of the Leicester Sketch Club, and a born teacher. He was an artist of the Old English School, which is basically using white or off-white paper and a limited range of colours, and so rich in knowledge and so generous in passing it on to his students.

The classrooms smelt of pencils, paper, rubbers, paint, and the like and I still clearly remember going into them and the individual smell that each had. I enjoyed every minute that I spent within the walls of the college. The normal procedure was for students to move through the various departments of the college, to enable them to get an appreciation of as many aspects of art as possible.

Much of the time in the first two or three terms was spent in the drawing class, under the direction of Mr Pop Atkins for whom I developed a great admiration. Pop wore a Norfolk jacket, knickerbockers which came to just below his knees, heavy knitted stockings, and country brogue shoes. While under his supervision we only used pencils. Mostly we drew still life objects in the classroom, but sometimes we went into Leicester which is well endowed with Norman and earlier buildings. Pop encouraged us to concentrate on doorways and decorative brick work, instilling in us the need for accuracy both in the image and its texture.

Back in the classrooms we were given a wide assortment of objects to draw. One of the first I remember was a plaster cast of a hand, borrowed from the sculpture class. Day after day we drew the same object, until our work was done to his satisfaction. At another time the class was drawing a plaster cast of a foot, and I took my sketch home to show my parents. About a month later my father asked what I had been doing that day, and I had to confess that I was still drawing the self-same foot. The reason for spending so much time on one object was beyond his understanding, but I did not find the seemingly endless repetition boring as I realised that all the time I was improving my artistic skill and sharpening my powers of observation of shapes, shades and textures. All this work was later to prove invaluable in my career as I became aware that it was no use being slick with a brush if the basic drawing lacked good imagery and perspective.

Gradually we moved through the classes. In the sculpture class most of us worked in clay or stone and only a few in wood. I preferred modelling in clay because it takes a relatively short time for the model to take shape and I liked the feel of wet smooth clay in my hand. A piece of sculpture, be it figure, or a bust, or an animal, has roundness and volume, which a sketch or painting lacks. Thus modelling helps the artist to appreciate depth and solidity of an object, which in turn helps him to convey a third dimension to his work.

When the models were finished, they were taken to the art room. Here Dan put them one at a time on a table and used them to illustrate the effect of light in creating dramatic highlights and shadows. In a dimly lit room, with the aid of candle held in various positions relative to the object, he demonstrated the intense, dramatic shadows thrown by a near light source. Then as it was taken further away the features became less pronounced, and the shadows more diffuse.

Before starting to draw or paint in the heraldry class we first had to study the history of the subject and to understand its grammar and laws. Shields made from plywood in the woodwork department were about four feet long and slightly bowed in the Norman style. They then went to the City and Guilds, painting and decorating class, where they were painted and rubbed down a number of times until they had a smooth matt finish, and were ready for us to complete. We each prepared a heraldic design to scale on paper. This was later transferred to a shield and painted on to it with enamel paints, these are strong colours and I particularly liked the gorgeous golds and blues. When I left college the shields which I had helped to make were displayed as a frieze round the top of the wall in the main hall, where they made a very impressive sight.

I also spent some time in the calligraphy class learning how to produce illuminated manuscripts. Each of us had a legend or a story to write in Gothic letters, with each capital illuminated by a small painting as a background to it.

There was a fine commercial section as many of the Leicester industries supported the college, and eventually gave employment to some of the students, in their department of commercial art or graphic art as it is known today. I remember in this class being set the task of producing a design for a hand cream jar, a label for it, and produce advertising material for market promotion. All the art work had to be of the highest quality for this purpose, and sound principles of design, presentation and colour were required. The class visited many factories to see what was being manufactured, and how they were already being promoted by the company.

I also enjoyed illustrating books as this gave the artist more freedom to express his interpretation of the scene which the author had described.

In the life class, an unadorned model was the usual subject, which made me aware of the beauty of the human figure and the subtle shadows which a shaft of light could throw across it. Considerable care was needed to get all parts of the body in their correct proportions, and to satisfactorily portray the

delicate skin texture. Whether painting or sketching, a model presents a strong challenge to the artist in producing a faithful portrait.

Throughout my three year course I was attending classes under the instruction of Dan Watson. In the classroom we painted an immense number of different objects. He was fond of natural subjects such as a bunch of spring flowers from his garden, or a sprig of blackberries, or an apple or two, or just a handful of wild flowers from a roadside verge. At another time he produced pieces of pottery such as jugs, vases, or ornaments, from his cupboard. When the fancy took him, he raided the domestic science block and borrowed things for us to draw much to the annoyance of the teacher if she found out before he managed to put them back.

Classroom time just seemed to fly past, and I was usually sorry when it was time to leave. In fact I was often the last to go, and then if I was lucky I walked home with Dan providing I could contrive to be at the gate as he came out. As we walked along we talked about art, and I asked questions about what we had been doing during the day and in this way I got extra tuition. He was somewhat absent minded, and I am sure he never really thought out in which direction I lived. Nearly every time that I walked with him, he asked 'Do you live in this direction boy?' to which I would reply rather hesitatingly 'Yes, er, yes that's right sir' praying that he would never discover that it was out of my way to accompany him. I so enjoyed listening and chatting to him, that I cared little for having to walk a long way round to get home. After we parted I would turn our conversation over in my mind and reconsider all that had been said and discussed.

On red-letter days, I was asked into his house. We went into the front parlour where he had a piano similar to that of my mother. Mrs Watson brought in afternoon tea consisting of very daintily cut sandwiches, cakes, and tea which we drank from small china cups. After we had finished our meal Dan would take some of his recent paintings from his portfolio, and one at a time prop them up on the music stand on the piano. Half talking to himself he then analysed and criticised each in turn. He made comments as to the strengths and weaknesses of the pictures, and how they could be improved with an extra patch of green or perhaps a stripe of brown. These sessions often lasted for over an hour and I listened entralled and learnt a great amount.

In Dan's pictures you could almost see the willows, the reeds and the grasses move. When he painted a landscape he conveyed the atmosphere, whether it was of clouds scudding across the sky, or of a still summer day without a breath of wind, or of an impending thunder storm from the heavy clouds in his sky.

He was principally a landscape artist and his students spent more time out of doors with him than on any other part of the course. In the classroom we were taught techniques we could use later when on a field day. From Dan I learned the science, joy, and subtlety of water-colours, which has had a lifelong influence on my work. When people say to me 'You paint in such a lovely low key with such delicate colours' I rejoice because I think to myself, that is the way in which my master taught me.

He enjoyed showing his students how to use textured paper, and the best way to apply washes to them. Dan had a curious habit of going into a shop when there was a sale on and buying a few rolls of wall paper for a penny or two each. On one side there was a hideous pattern but this was of no concern to him, as he was only interested in the reverse side which had to be a near white or fawn for him to buy the roll. After cutting a roll into manageable pieces he used them for watercolour painting. He painted strong pictures in burnt umber, blue or green, at the same time using the colour of the paper for any appropriate object. To him the paper colour was an integral part of the painting as the need to cover every inch of paper with paint was not necessary in his opinion.

For another demonstration he took a sheet of paper and immersed it in water until it was thoroughly soaked. Then he put it on a plate glass table and while it was still very wet applied water-colour washes to it with a large sable brush. We students crowded round to watch which of the colours separated out or which merged together. At various stages as the paper dried he showed us how to judge just when to apply more paint and how to get them to blend together to get a desired effect. It was at classes like this that I felt excited and thrilled when seeing the wonderful result which a real master of his art could obtain with such basic materials.

In the classroom I spent many hours developing skills which I have used regularly ever since. I enjoyed painting landscapes and with Dan's help improved my pictures by applying some of the fundamental principles to them. He had me painting in tones of one colour to develop an understanding of aerial perspective. The idea is to indicate distance through using different tones of colour. The reason why this can be done is that colours in the foreground are dark and gradually get lighter as they recede into the distance.

Dan would say 'I want you to convey 5 miles in a ¼ inch'. Then using tones of any colour I cared to choose I worked to produce the illusion of distance on the narrow piece of paper he had provided. When he was satisfied he said 'Now do 5 miles in ⅛ inch'. He was a hard task master but I have never regretted the time that I slaved away trying to please him, by producing the end result to the best of my ability.

When I was having difficulty with a picture Dan would say 'Don't worry son, turn its face to the wall, put it away'. Then two or three days later he would say 'Get it out and let's have look at it'. When it had been turned round we examined it with

An early water-colour. Fields near Enderby, 1936

what he referred to as 'fresh' eyes, and usually I could see immediately why I had been worried. Perhaps a tree or a building did not look right, and Dan was able to point out why and also indicate how I could correct it.

Sometimes when he looked at a picture that I was working on he would ask 'Do you really think the grass is that colour?'. Then to emphasise his point I would be sent out to collect some grass to put on to the painting. This usually showed how raw my yellowish green was when seen against the soft natural green. 'Get some mud into it' he would say indicating that I should add some burnt sienna to the green. Gradually I learnt to make greens without bright yellow, and to study natural colours more carefully. One of Dan's favourite sayings was that nature never makes a mistake with its colours, all of which blend together in the countryside.

As a picture developed he would help with its composition showing how it might be improved by putting in an extra figure or tree. His expression which I have never forgotten was 'Drop a figure or an animal into the landscape to heighten the interest and improve the composition'.

Apart from the days spent in the field with classes from the college, I often had the privilege of going out with Dan at the weekends. Together we walked through the water meadows along the River Soar to find suitable subjects. Usually they were composed of meadows with cattle or sheep, willow trees, and tall vegetation growing beside the course of one of the many ditches which ran through the fields. He never tired of talking about willow trees, how light caught the soft dirty green of the leaves and then the contrasting silvery grey of the underside. These landscapes became, and remain my favourite, both for walking through and for painting. I learned to observe the countryside as I walked through it, and found that by addressing myself to it, windows and doors were opened and I could find an endless supply of subjects where-ever I happened to be.

We did not limit ourselves to the meadows, and for a change we sometimes visited Charnwood Forest which was another of Dan's favourite areas. This was a wilder type of countryside, covered with bracken, pine trees, and outcrops of hard purplish granite. We visited Bradgate Park on many occasions to paint the beautiful ruins of what was called 'Lady Jane Grey's house. These lovely Elizabethan red brick ruins, sur-rounded by trees, provided some good subjects as did the deer, and rocky outcrops in the park.

On other days we walked along the canal and river banks, to paint locks with their decaying wooden gates, and well worn posts where generations of bargees had tied their craft while they waited their turn to go through or perhaps refreshed themselves at the pub. Never far away on these days were the cattle, belly deep in grass in the meadows, and the smell of meadowsweet.

Dan sat on a small stool

When he was painting in the field Dan sat on a small stool, with his paper, mounted on a board, balanced on his knees. I was taught in this way and whenever I am working out of doors still use this method because it is so easy to control the washes by slight adjustments to the slope of the board.

He used an old white dinner plate for mixing his paint on, and I still do exactly the same with an old enamel plate that I bought many years ago for a few pence. It goes everywhere with me whether I am demonstrating to a WI meeting, on holiday, or visiting another part of the country, or just having a day painting. Water he carried in a medicine bottle, and his brushes in a holder made from a section of bamboo cane about an inch in diameter, with a cork in each end. All his equipment was carried in a small case, which combined with his style of dress made his resemblance to a bank manager even more striking.

Dan took me to a number of art galleries to study the compositions and skills of a wide range of other artists. We went to the Museum at Kettering to see the magnificent canvasses of Sir Alfred East, to Lincoln to study Peter de Wint's work, and to Nottingham to see the paintings of Sir Arnesby Brown who worked for many years in his native Nottinghamshire before settling in Norfolk. I particularly admired the wonderful skies of Sir Arnesby Brown's Norfolk paintings, and have since spent a considerable amount of time working in the same area of the county where he did most of his work.

I spent many joyful days with Dan. His enthusiasm for water-colours was infectious, and I soon realised after I started to attend the college that I wanted to spend my life working in this wonderful but challenging medium. Art has been a gratifying way of life for me and I shall always be thankful to the men who were my tutors and especially to Dan, who opened vistas which have enriched my life.

Canal bridge and barge

CHAPTER 4

Royal Navy

In the autumn of 1939 I received my 'calling up' papers instructing me to report to Butlins Holiday camp at Skegness. Training in the Royal Navy at that time was rather chaotic. All suitable venues had been requisitioned, as the regular barracks and training ships could not cope with the large influx of new recruits.

January 1940 was bitterly cold with heavy snow and arctic winds blowing off the North Sea. The chalets where we were housed were only built for summer use, and consequently the walls were thin and not insulated and I spent many a cold night there. Added to this my uniform was ill-fitting and not thick enough to keep me warm. It was a spartan existence which was preparing me for the rigours ahead, of which I was blissfully unaware at the time.

At this camp I experienced my first taste of real war, when some of my fellow sailors and I came under attack from a German aircraft. I was part of a squad engaged in scraping paper labels from empty tins so that they could be sent back as scrap for melting down and re-use. This was a thankless task but was all part of the 'war effort' on which everyone was engaged.

We heard an aircraft approaching from over the dunes but as we had no idea of aircraft identification, were not aware that it was an enemy plane until we heard the sound of machine guns. As I dived over a wall, landing amongst the waste bins from the cookhouse, I could hear the bullets rattling the tins, which were jumping up and down like hot potatoes.

From Skegness I went to Portsmouth where I spent a few more weeks training and square bashing before being selected for sea going duties. I learned that I had been drafted to join the crew of HMS Oribi, lying at Scapa Flow. The journey by train from nearly one end of the country to the other took two days. It was all very bewildering as we were still rather raw sailors, unused to travelling long distances on slow-moving trains, and of course we were apprehensive about going to sea.

The train took us to Scrabster, where we caught a ferry called the 'St. Ninian' which took us across the Pentland Firth to join our ships. The Pentland Firth is a stretch of sea between the extreme north of Scotland and the Orkneys, where the

HMS Oribi at Scapa Flow

Atlantic and the North Sea meet. This is enough to create turbulence but if there is also a strong wind, as there was when we crossed, then the sea is very rough. The ferry was so crowded, every available space being filled, that I spent much of the time on the upper deck. We nosed our way out of the protection of the harbour walls and very soon the old ferry met the choppy seas and began to dig her bow into the waves, taking water over the deck as a consequence.

The crossing took two hours, many of us were seasick and we must have looked a sorry sight as we waited on deck for the ships' boats to come alongside and take us to our respective warships.

Scapa Flow seemed full of naval vessels, both large and small, lying anchored to metal buoys. HMS Oribi was a long sleek destroyer painted in Navy grey with a short stubby funnel. She looked powerful. I had my hammock slung over my shoulder, and my clothes in a canvas sea bag. The clothes I was wearing were wet, and after the terrible ferry crossing I felt very unhappy as I followed one of the crew to my quarters in the forward part of the ship. After a day or two on board I was allocated my duties in the engine room, and soon began to feel a part of the crew.

I had not been long aboard when there was a noticeable increase in activity. Engines were started, creating noise which was completely new to me, and it was not long before I realised that we were preparing to go to sea. Our duty was to join other naval ships to escort a convoy of merchantmen to Murmansk. This was the start of over two years that I spent on Russian convoys to Archangel and Murmansk.

It was quite an experience, with days on end at sea in almost constant daylight and sometimes in near perpetual darkness. My first days at sea were filled with excitement. Whenever I was on deck I marvelled at the vast expanse of water, the flatness and the dramatic light in the sky above. There was an openness and apparent peacefulness as I set off on my first voyage. It was not until I witnessed the devastating effect of a torpedo attack that this sense of wonderment left me and the reality of war returned.

In the long summer nights when the sun never really set, the sky would sometimes be filled with the aurora borealis, or northern lights. It seemed as if light was being reflected from

First Class Stoker Certificate issued aboard the depot ship HMS Tyne

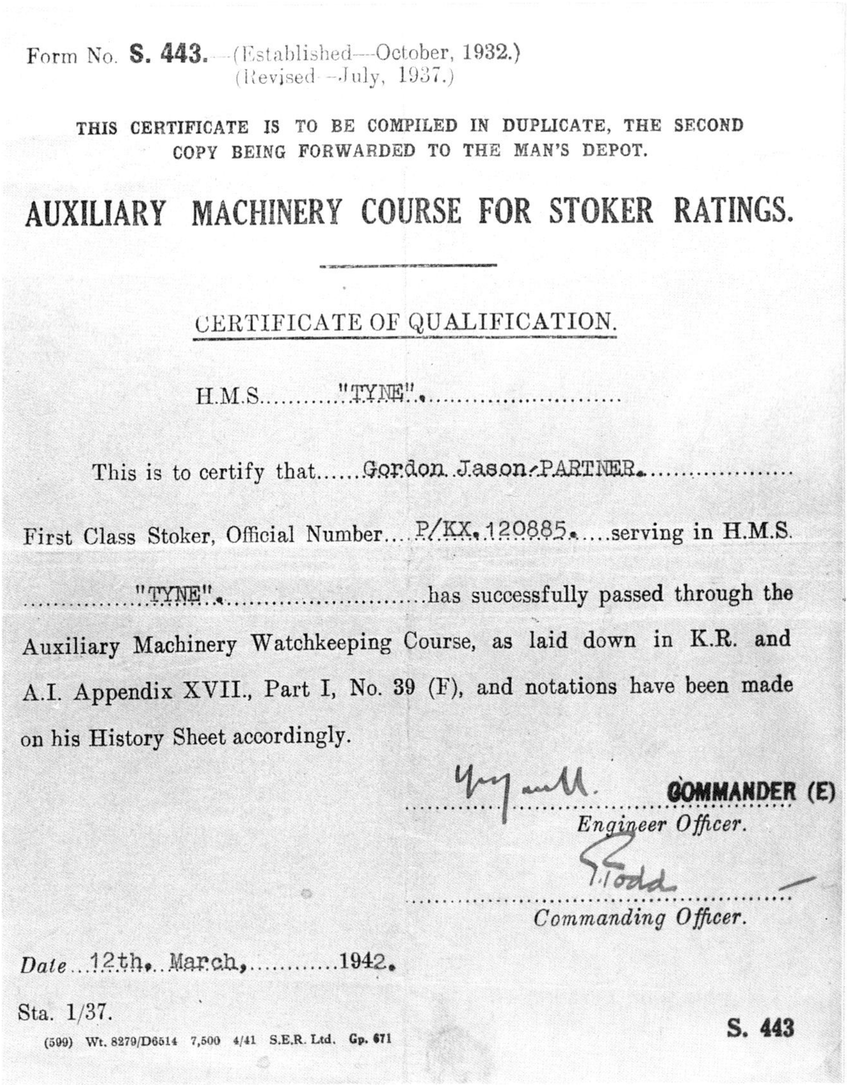

Form No. **S. 443.** (Established—October, 1932.)
(Revised—July, 1937.)

THIS CERTIFICATE IS TO BE COMPILED IN DUPLICATE, THE SECOND COPY BEING FORWARDED TO THE MAN'S DEPOT.

AUXILIARY MACHINERY COURSE FOR STOKER RATINGS.

CERTIFICATE OF QUALIFICATION.

H.M.S. "TYNE".

This is to certify that Gordon Jason PARTNER.

First Class Stoker, Official Number P/KX. 120885. serving in H.M.S.

"TYNE". has successfully passed through the

Auxiliary Machinery Watchkeeping Course, as laid down in K.R. and

A.I. Appendix XVII., Part I, No. 39 (F), and notations have been made

on his History Sheet accordingly.

COMMANDER (E)
Engineer Officer.

Commanding Officer.

Date 12th. March, 1942.

Sta. 1/37.

(599) Wt. 8279/D6514 7,500 4/41 S.E.R. Ltd. Gp. 671

S. 443

the polar ice into the sky, illuminating and colouring the clouds in a fantastic, awe-inspiring display. As I watched, I thought of primitive men witnessing the phenomenon and how frightened they would understandably have been. They might well have believed the sight to be the work of the devil. For much of the summer months there were only two or three hours of darkness.

But oh! the interminable unending darkness of winter. The intense cold added to the misery of winter convoys. I have known the temperature to fall to 47°F below zero. At these times, as the sea broke along the ship's side, the edges of the waves froze and the superstructure and rigging became so heavy with ice that it threatened the stability of the ship. Despite the cold we had to go on deck and chip the ice away with hammers and iron bars. Wrapped in duffle coats, bala-clava helmets and scarves, we did our best to chip some of the tons of ice away as the ship pitched and rolled. Clothed in ice she looked more like a ghost ship than destroyer. There was so much ice that if it was not removed, the point of balance could

Aboard HMS Oribi on Russian convoy duty (author on the left)

be displaced and there was a danger of capsizing. Some of the guns could not be operated because of the cold as they were not electrically heated at the time. The lubricating oil became so viscous at the low temperature that it was impossible to move them in any direction. It was usual to work for half an hour, or an hour at most before returning below. Even in this time eyebrows, moustaches and beards were whitened with frost.

Down below it was warm, but very humid, as every opening had to be kept closed to conserve heat. The atmosphere was so damp that water dripped from the bulkheads and our clothes never seemed dry. These unpleasant conditions caused illness from chest complaints among the crew, some of whom later developed tuberculosis. We were young then, fighting a war, and living conditions were the least of our problems.

It took about fourteen days from the time that the convoy had collected together to docking in Russia. All the time the Royal Navy vessels maintained watch to try to protect the merchant ships from the constant danger of a U-boat attack. As the cargo ships plodded away, we fussed around them like nurses looking after their charges. Progress of the convoy was determined by the speed of the slowest vessel and if any ship developed engine trouble and began to fall behind, it became a worry to the convoy commander, as it could be so easily singled out for a U-boat attack. In good weather, during daylight, it was possible to keep in visual contact with other ships in the convoy, but when it was stormy and dark for days on end, no other ship might be spotted.

Sometimes ships would disappear as a snow shower swept across our path. Then there would be a break and, almost as if by magic, they would reappear in the distance. I developed a great respect for the merchant navy during those voyages, as despite the weather and the roughness of the seas, they did their utmost to maintain their station in the convoy.

Although the convoy changed course from time to time by swinging to port and sailing for a few hours, and then swinging to starboard for a few hours, we were not able to avoid U-boat attacks. At first, the boats hunted individually but later they hunted in what we called 'wolf packs'. We lost many of our ships from these convoys.

At any time during the day or night, there might be a dull thud, signalling that a torpedo had struck, sending the sailors on board to a watery grave. Very few were lucky enough to be picked up alive, as it was not possible to survive for more than a few minutes in the icy water.

We were fortunate to survive a torpedo attack and managed to sink the U-boat and capture its captain. Under interrogation he admitted that he had fired two torpedos but they had gone under the ship. He had not identified us as a destroyer and thought that we were a much larger ship with a much greater depth below the waterline and had set his torpedos so deep that they went right under our ship.

*Royal Navy Commando
Combined Operations*

As we approached the Russian ports in the wintertime, we were met by an ice breaker, which we all followed in close line astern before the ice was able to reform. For two or three days, while the cargoes were being unloaded, we were at anchor and could get some much needed sleep and get our clothes dry.

The arms carried by the convoys were desperately needed by the Russian army. On one occasion, when the German army was advancing towards Leningrad, soldiers were waiting at the quayside to drive the tanks straight off the ships into battle.

After two years on the convoys, during a period of shore duty, I happened to see a notice asking for volunteers for combined operations. I had no idea what this involved but felt that anything would be an improvement on the discomfort of being at sea and, without asking any questions, I added my name to the list.

I did not have to wait long before finding out why combined operations units were being formed. They were designed to spearhead the invasion into Europe and were manned partly by soldiers and partly by sailors. The idea was that sailors with sea-going experience would be able to handle the landing craft while crossing the English Channel. I was absorbed into a unit of the Royal Marine Commandos and was posted to Troon in Ayrshire.

Here I spent several weeks in intensive training in various parts of the west coast of Scotland. This was ideal training territory as we could practice amphibious landings on the islands off the coast and on the mainland, wherever there was a suitable beach away from the prying eyes of enemy reconnaissance aircraft. We were also given basic training in rock climbing and in commando techniques.

'Yomping' in the Scottish highlands

After a few months of basic training, the unit was transferred to our base camp near Oban. From there we practised landing on various other islands, scaling rocks and cliffs to get a foothold on the countryside. For general toughening and endurance training, we went on long marches. I particularly remember the countryside around Rothesay, which was beautiful in the spring, with its woods of larch and silver birch and banks of wild daffodils. Then there were the mountain streams with their crystal clear water, sparkling in the sun as they tumbled over the rock strewn river beds.

On several occasions we went on 2- or 3-day marches which involved bivouacing, or just sheltering as best we could under branches over which some bracken was thrown for extra protection. We had some army cooks and butchers with us and were instructed in how to live off the countryside. We first had to catch a sheep, then we were shown how to kill it. We then cooked it over an open fire and it tasted delicious. I often wondered whether the farmer was compensated for the sheep we ate.

It was a rough life but I became very fit and could meet the physical requirements without any great difficulty. We were lucky to be in such a spectacular area, living close to nature, and I thoroughly enjoyed it. I managed to buy a few packs of postcards on which I could draw and make a few notes during the infrequent moments of relaxation we had. How I longed to have a sketchbook and plenty of time to fill it.

The unit spent periods of varying lengths on several of the Western Isles. We visited Iona with its beautiful cathedral ruins and although I was engrossed in training for war, I could still appreciate and enjoy the wild openness of the islands and the sea around them. The water was so clear that it reflected the blue and green shades of the rocks, and across the bays and inlets, nestling in the hills, were little white crofts, seemingly scattered at random and sometimes miles apart from each other.

As the number of troops increased in preparation for the invasion, it became increasingly difficult to accommodate everyone in army camps. Our unit was moved to the Ardnamurchan peninsular where some of us had to be billeted with local families. I thought it was marvellous to have the chance to live with a family rather than share a nissen hut with 20 or 30 other soldiers.

One day a detachment of us went out in a lorry, with a sergeant in charge, to look for people willing to provide lodgings. Many of the small communities of crofts consisted of only a few houses and not many of the other soldiers were willing to accept lodgings in them. They preferred larger villages where there was a least a public house.

I was not displeased when my turn came to accept lodgings with a Mrs. Gillespie. Her small croft was one of five located near Glenborrodale, down a track nearly a mile long, which was unsuitable for motor vehicles. After travelling about three miles along a lonely road in the lorry, I found myself dropped off with my kitbag and sleeping gear and having to walk to Mrs. Gillespie's croft. The track was hardly more than a peaty footpath which zig-zagged for about half a mile through the heather until it crossed a burn about four feet wide. There was no bridge, just stepping stones, which were adequate for most of the time but after heavy rain when the water level rose it was impossible to get across without getting wet unless wearing waders.

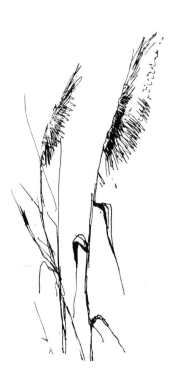

A little further down where the valley opened out, the crofts became visible and beyond them was a bay with a beach of silver sand. I could not carry all my gear in one go and as I went back up again I saw for the first time the open moorland above the road and the bronze mixture of bracken and heather.

Mrs. Gillespie's croft was a single storey dwelling with white painted walls and corrugated iron roof. There was a small outhouse attached where a cow was kept, and in the yard there were a few chickens running about. A little further up the hill there were a few small enclosures where the cows were tethered during the day, and where enough hay could be made to feed the animals during the winter.

Inside there was an open grate in which a peat fire burned night and day. As far as I could ascertain it was allowed to go out sometime in the spring and then it was re-lit in a traditional way to start the new year. All the cooking was done on the range and there was the ever-present acrid smell of burning peat throughout the house.

To one side of the fireplace there was a hole in the wall about three feet deep and long enough for a mattress. This was my bed and after I had retired for the night I drew the curtains across until morning. It was very comfortable and many a night I stayed awake listening to the sighing of the winds which were so persistent and strong that the small scrubby trees were bent in a west to easterly direction. On other evenings I could hear waves beating on the shore and the call of sea birds and waders. The summer evenings were light well into the night, although not quite like the midnight sun of the Russian convoys. Winter evenings were very long and the days short.

Mrs. Gillespie's cottage. An early oil painting which was subsequently used for a calendar

Mrs. Gillespie was a widow and always wore black clothes. Her hair was plaited into circular buns which covered her ears, resembling ear muffs, similar to those I remembered in Leicestershire before the war. At first her broad Scots' accent was like a foreign language to me but gradually I became accustomed to it. Initially I felt very much apart. Conversation among the crofters, most of whom were related to Mrs. Gillespie, was confined to 'Good morning' or 'Good evening' but slowly I was absorbed into the community and eventually I began to feel at home.

The men got a living by fishing in the bay during the spring and summer. After a day out at sea they sailed over to a small village beyond the headland of the bay where there was a slip-way convenient for unloading and selling the fish. Sometimes they spent the day gathering seaweed, which was stacked up to rot down for eventual use as a fertiliser for their small kitchen gardens.

Whenever I could I went down to the beach. Sometimes I wandered along to see what I could find among the stones and

Low water at Thornham

shells of the shoreline. It was an excellent coast for beach-combing and there was a local feeling that if anything was needed, sooner or later it would be washed up. Timber arrived in profusion, anything from crates to large planks, which required two men to carry. The crofters satisfied all their needs for making gates, doors or furniture from the sea, and there was always an abundance of firewood to supplement the peat dug from the moors.

My sketching and painting was restricted by the lack of materials. I soon exhausted my limited supply of postcards and had to resort to the serviceman's method of 'acquiring' some paper. I managed to find a piece of plywood and a paper clip. this was followed by 'acquiring' some paper, after which I was in a position to start drawing again. I ended up with a collection of my work which had Admiralty memos or routine orders on the reverse side. It was a wonderful area for painting and I spent every daylight hour that I could, exploring subjects both on the coastline and on the moors.

Mrs. Gillespie did her shopping in the post office and general stores across the bay. Once a week one of her relations would row over to the village to pick up her letters and groceries. As winter approached she tried to build up her stock of food against the time when the crofts would be cut off by snow and the seas too rough to cross. Although she was allocated extra rations for feeding me, it was extremely difficult to buy ahead as she had been accustomed to do in peacetime.

On most days I was picked up by a lorry and taken to the camp to continue my military training. It was a continuous routine of marching and practising over obstacle courses, to keep our bodies fit and alert. This was interspersed with lectures on our equipment, guns, landing craft and tactics on the battlefield.

I got to know when I was needed at camp so that sometimes I did not show up there for two or three days. If I was required on parade then one of the platoon had to come down the track to fetch me while the lorry waited. Like all servicemen I began to carve a niche for myself and was thoroughly happy in my peaceful little haven among the bracken and heather.

One day when I was on the camp, the CO, a Colonel Harcourt, known to us all as Judd, took me aside and asked me if I was all right. I think he was concerned that although many of the platoons had moved on to other camps, I had managed to stay there. He was worried that I might be getting too isolated, losing my rapport with humanity and in danger of becoming a recluse. I soon assured him of my happiness and pointed out that whilst I enjoyed the solitude of my lodgings and surroundings, I was not in the least lonely.

There is a vast difference between solitude and loneliness in an artist's life. Whilst I was enjoying the solitude I felt that my soul was free and at peace with my surroundings which provided me with the inspiration and subjects for my artistic needs. I was often more lonely when on camp in the midst of other soldiers, preparing for war, where my soul was numb and the world around me provided no inspiration or relief from the tedium of army life. I do not think I managed to convince the CO of my feelings and for the rest of my stay there I felt I was treated as the pet artist who was rather eccentric, but harmless and should be humoured as much as possible.

All too soon for me, the time inevitably arrived when our unit moved to one of the islands. Here again, I lived in a small community where the easiest access was from the sea. Once a week, all the housewives, dressed in their overcoats, bonnets, scarves and wellies, gathered on the beach waiting for the ferry to take them to a large village on the other side of the bay. This had a landing stage and the ladies, conscious of wishing to make a good appearance, sat on a wall and changed their wellies for town shoes before they set off for the shops.

On their return they again donned their wellies in preparation for the landing back home, which had to be made on the beach wherever the state of the tide permitted. The men jumped ashore and hauled the boat up the beach as far as they could, before helping the ladies off. Then everybody formed a human chain to unload the shopping. Everything from a roll of lino to a tin of paraffin, or the week's groceries had to be handled in this way. At the end of it all everyone knew what everyone else had bought but this did not worry anyone. The whole expedition was accepted as part of their unchanging way of life.

On this island I first became aware of the beauty of the bagpipes. One of my landlady's relatives had a habit of playing them in the evening and, frequently, well into the night. No unnatural sound interfered with his playing, there was just the sound of the sea or wind, or the call of sea birds. I grew to love the haunting sound of the pipes as the melodies floated across the countryside.

For much of the time at this camp we were engaged in making roads. They were only rough tracks made from local rocks, which we broke with 7lb hammers, making our party resemble the chain gangs seen on films before the war. Gradually the roads were extended and our marches to and from work each morning and evening also grew longer, until we were walking at least five miles each way.

Most of the way back we were allowed to march at ease, which meant we could talk and smoke, but as we approached the camp entrance we were called to attention. Arms moved smartly forward and back in unison with our steps and occasionally from within the camp came the sound of bagpipes. After a long exhausting day, these sounded magical to me. Over the camp entrance, supported by pine poles cut from the forest, was a board with the name of the camp. It always reminded me of a confederate patrol returning to camp, as portrayed in a western film. At the side of the road,

Camp

somebody with a sense of humour, had made a grave complete with gravestone on which was written 'Here lies Private Atkins. He was a brave soldier but he forgot to duck'. This puzzled me for quite a long time until we were taken out on manoeuvres on the moorlands, with live ammunition. We had to crawl over the ground as bullets whistled overhead. Only then did I realise that to keep your head down was the only way to survive, no matter how uncomfortable it was to go through prickly heather or flooded bog.

Imagine working in the open air, doing hard physical work, getting just corned beef sandwiches with only a scraping of butter on the bread and a mug of tea. Our appetites were enormous but all that awaited us was the simplest and most meagre meal. Typically, we had some 'Spam' with perhaps some pickle and a slice of bread. I was perpetually hungry but food was so short and so strictly rationed that there was nothing else available.

On Sundays we went on church parades and as we marched along to the accompaniment of a pipe band, the sound seemed to fill and reverberate through the small glens. It stirred my heart and even today their sound sends shivers down my spine as I recall this interlude which was all so peaceful but only to last a few short months before the real carnage and destruction of war was upon us.

There came a time when rumours of our moving south were rife within the camp. With a mixture of exhilaration and fear we began to load our lorries with equipment and our personal belongings in a single kitbag to start our embarkation to the mainland. Long lines of camouflaged lorries slowly started to fill roads leading to the south of England. Railway lines must have become choked with troop trains making their way in the same direction. We all became acutely aware that preparations were afoot for the invasion of Europe and it was only a matter of time before the years of training would be used to good effect. Practising was over and now it was to be the real thing and it was to be a fight for survival.

After over two days on the train, our unit eventually arrived in the New Forest. There could not have been a greater contrast with the solitude and quiet of the Western Isles. Here there was always something happening as the concentration of troops built up, with lorries coming and going all day long, and often well into the night. We were amongst thousands of troops of many nationalities. Tanks, Bren gun carriers, guns, lorries and every conceivable type of military equipment filled almost the whole forest. There were great stacks of boxes of ammunition, everything shrouded in camouflage nets to avoid detection by enemy aircraft.

Most of our waking hours were occupied with training activities. We marched miles, both by day and night. Very early one morning, when we were returning to camp after an all-night march, we startled an early riser in one of the cottages. Dressed in camouflaged uniform, green berets and thick rubber-soled commando boots, she did not see or hear us approach. To add to our disguise we had blackened our faces with charred cork. The frightened woman screamed as she rushed back into her cottage. Soon, everybody became accustomed to seeing troops throughout the day and night and went about their daily tasks, hardly taking any notice of us.

Our camp was near Emery Down and occasionally it was possible to get down to the 'local' in the evening. Beer was not very plentiful and it was rationed to a pint each on most nights. Here I met a grand old man of the forest called Sonny. He must have been between 70 and 80 and his knarled hands showed that he had lived a hard outdoor life. When I saw him there I used to persuade the barmaid to let me have a pint for him. As he was a local she normally obliged unless the barrel was nearly empty. He always accepted graciously and although he clasped the glass with both hands, it shook uncontrollably as he lifted it to his mouth. I spent hours listening to him talk about the New Forest, of the wild deer and ponies, and how things had changed during his lifetime. He had been a woodcutter and still had the right to cut trees for firewood, providing they were no thicker than a man's wrist. The quiet times I spent with Sonny made me forget momentarily about war.

Although we had no idea of the date of D-Day, its approach was obviously getting closer. We were confined to camp more frequently and for longer periods, and it was almost

impossible to get a 24-hour pass to visit friends or relatives.

From time to time, detachments of troops were sent down to Stokes Bay where landing craft were being assembled. We practised loading troops and equipment, getting everyone into a state of alertness. Sometimes we would have to remain on board for several hours before disembarking and returning back to camp. I was known to many of the officers as an artist and in quieter moments I was called up to the bridge and asked to paint a pin-up on the superstructure. These became symbols for the craft in much the same way as aircrews had pin-ups on the side of their aircraft.

A Canadian officer noticed me at work one day and asked if I could so some painting for him. His flotilla was alongside ours and seeing me at work had inspired him to make his boats look like sharks. He managed to acquire some paint and I was soon busy painting the shark's open red mouth surrounded by jagged teeth on the bows of the boats under his command. To add further to the illusion, the anchor hole was painted black with a white surround, to resemble an eye. The effect was quite striking and he was so pleased that I managed to get a pass home to see my parents. This was the only time in the services that I managed to get any reward for my talents. In the event, this was the last time I got home before D-Day.

Gradually the tension grew as we spent more and more time squeezed, like sardines, into the landing craft. We never knew at the time what was happening but now, of course, know that General Eisenhower, who had his headquarters a short distance away behind Portsmouth, was waiting for favourable weather and seas before giving the command to invade.

To relieve tension I managed to obtain some paper so that I could while away idle moments with a little sketching. I drew the landing craft so often that they were instilled in my memory and I can still draw them to this day. One day, forgetting myself, I climbed on to the forward deck to get a different angle on the scene. Two military policemen soon descended on me and I was marched off to my commanding officer. They were worried that I might be a spy making notes but fortunately the CO knew me and after a due warning told me not to do that again.

At this time we began to get briefing lectures of the landing areas. For this purpose, models had been constructed, using all the information which could be scraped together, including holiday information and postcards, for which a general appeal had gone out much earlier. The basic information was supplemented as fully as possible with aerial reconnaissance indicating where the heaviest fortifications had been constructed. Time and again we went through these briefing sessions until we felt we could land on the beach and find our way up it even when blindfolded.

In early June 1944, we became convinced that the invasion was not far away. We all wrote letters to our families 'just in case' and gave them to friends or the padre. The landing craft were loaded on 5th June for what was to be the last time and in the evening, we departed.

To actually be moving was a relief, whatever awaited us on

The Canadian flotilla of 'sharks'

the other side. There was no turning back now and I think we all felt that this was the beginning of the end of the war but how far away this was, we had no conceiveable way of knowing.

Throughout the night and early morning the sky was full of aircraft. On our voyage, as the bombardment intensified and we approached the coast of France, we could see the flashes of explosions and eventually the sound of bombing above the throbbing noise of our engine. We became aware of all sorts of aircraft, which we could recognise as fighters, bombers or troop carriers loaded with contingents of airborne soldiers. There were also huge gliders being towed slowly across.

As we approached we began to witness the inferno of war. The anti-aircraft flak and enemy fighters were attacking our aircraft, sending some of them plummeting to the ground in flames.

I survived the landings and went through France, Holland and, eventually, into part of Germany. I bore witness to man's inhumanity to his fellow man, and saw beautiful old cities bombed into ruins and fine works of art and architecture wantonly destroyed. I was saddened and sickened by the destruction I saw. When I heard the news of the cease-fire I felt that at last I could relax a little and hoped that I had fought in the war to end all wars.

Naval message instructing Patrol Leader Partner 'N' squad to attack pillbox west of centre beach head. Hold farmhouse 100 yards north and then to rejoin 'K' patrol and to leave wounded in pillbox 'A'
Operation Neptune was the code name for the European invasion

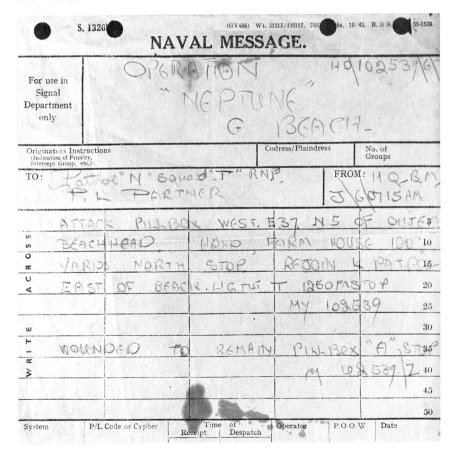

CHAPTER 5

Commercial Artist

After about six years in the Services, I was over-joyed to be drafted back to Portsmouth, as I was quite convinced that it was then only a matter of time before I would be demobbed. There was a much happier atmosphere than when I had been there before. The blackout had long since been abandoned and instead of having to grobe around in the dark, the camp was fully lit and seemed more like Piccadilly Circus than a navy camp. Some of the shortages were less acute and there was no need to be hungry as there was always food to be bought in the NAAFI.

Each night there was merry gathering somewhere on the camp as groups of men and women were having their last drinks together before being demobbed. Daily, everyone went to look at the demob list to see if his or her name had appeared.

Although I had served most of my time in combined operations I was still considered to be a Royal Navy sailor. There were not many of us who only had a khaki uniform and I felt rather conspicuous when on parade amongst the sailors. In the records I remained a sailor and one day, to my horror, I discovered that far from being demobbed I had been drafted to a ship due to leave shortly for Singapore!

I hastened to see the drafting officer to explain that it was four years since I had actually sailed in a warship. But he was not interested. As far as he was concerned I was an engine room sailor on my way to Singapore. No notice was taken of my vigorous protests and shortly afterwards, I was sent to Glasgow to join the ship.

When I was on board I repeated my story as often as I could to anybody who I thought might be able to help, but all to no avail I still had no naval kit but this did not seem to be a concern to anybody.

We set sail from Glasgow with me in the depths of despair, not knowing how long it would take to reach Singapore and back home again.

Fortunately the ship made a scheduled stop at Southampton for refuelling and taking on supplies. During the short stop, while I was on deck, I suddenly became aware that my name was being called over the Tannoy instructing me to report to the Master of Arms. There I received the glad tidings that there had been a mistake. I was due to be demobbed and was instructed to collect my kit and get ashore as soon as possible. From Southampton I was drafted to Lowestoft, from where I was eventually demobbed.

Inside a large hangar-like building we were issued with our demob clothing but before this, we had to pass a table at which a Colour Sergeant Royal Marines was seated, trying to persuade sailors to sign on for a period in the regular Navy and Marines. A few of my companions did show some interest but I did not stay long enough to see whether any decided to sign on.

I can remember accumulating a suit, shirts, underwear and shoes in my arms and then getting to where the trilby hats were being given out 'Size' shouted the burly sergeant. 'It's all right' I said, 'I don't want a trilby, in fact I never wear a hat.' 'Size' came the reply I explained again, thinking that he had not heard the first time. He was determined that I should have a hat, picked one up from his pile and pressed in on top of my other clothes. There was only one other item remaining to be collected and that was a cardboard box to contain my newly acquired wardrobe. The corporal balanced this as best he could on the clothes and I stumbled along trying to find a clear space to put everything down so that I could start packing.

A tall Colour Sergeant approached me and with a grin on his face asked sarcastically 'Can I help you sailor?'. I thought for a

'The Colour Sergeant asked if he could help'

moment before replying, 'Yes sarge, you can pack my box for me'. His face was a picture, his cheeks turned puce, and he must have been so flabbergasted by my audacity that he bent down and neatly packed my clothes as I handed them to him.

It was absolutely wonderful being on the train. Going across the Acle marshes I had no thoughts that I would return to them frequently in future years, to paint the open East Anglian scenes. Although I loved the countryside I had only one thought on my mind at that time and that was how I should be able to make a living.

My first thoughts were of Dan and the college. I had kept in touch with him during the war and I knew that, in spite of his advancing years, he was still teaching. Had it not been for the war and the shortage of teachers, he would have retired several years earlier.

My thoughts returned to a conversation that we had a short time before I left for the Navy. Dan was in a philosophical and contemplative mood. 'Well young man, it looks as if you are going to be a water-colour painter', he said, and then continued 'I would just like to give you a few words of advice, as it would seem that with hard work and some luck, you will be able to earn your living as an artist'. I felt very flattered that my mentor should give me this amount of encouragement and managed to say, while he paused in his thoughts, 'That is what I dream of, sir'.

He probably did not hear what I had said but went on, 'You will have a certain talent but do not assume that it is yours by right. Try to think of it as a gift, albeit a wonderful gift, but bear in mind it is bestowed on you almost like an honour. Imagine it is a cloak which I have chosen for you to wear. I will be passing it on to you and it is my privilege and duty to instruct you how to wear it and not to abuse or dishonour it by greed'.

After a short reflective pause, he continued, 'While I have had the privilege to wear it, I have known the joys that it can bring, for an artist can fully appreciate the rising sun at dawn, the wind in the trees, the light on the fields and the cattle in the meadows. The more you observe nature the greater your vision of the countryside becomes. You will be fulfilled with the magic of painting, and through your painting you will open vistas to others, whether they are also artists or not'.

'But try at all times to pay homage to nature through the sincerity and interity of your art. You may think you are a good artist, some people may think that you are very good and buy your paintings but never let this affect your work. Remember always the cloak you are wearing'.

At the time I was taken aback by this homily from the master for whom I had such a high regard. I could think of no way to comment, and he continued, 'In time, when you are fortunate enough to be professional artist, the time will come when you will be able to assist others to wear the cloak. Maybe a member of your family will wear it or it may be a student but whoever it is, share your knowledge so that he or she will wear the cloak with honour'.

I managed to say, 'Yes, but if I am able to earn a living I will have to sell my paintings'. 'Yes indeed' he said, 'We are living in a material world and you will need money but always charge for your work with a sense of fairness and integrity. If your work is sought after, do not overcharge your clients but remember it is your privilege to be able to earn a living by painting'.

'When you are successful many people will envy you but do not let your success turn your head to the extent that you think you can do everything. Forget your ego and be humble in the face of nature. In this way you will find that you retain the magic of painting and you will have, for all your life, a thrill when you pick up your brushes and start to paint the wonders of the countryside around you'.

This sounded very poetical at the time but it made a very deep impression on me and had a profound effect on my attitude to life. I have always believed in what Dan told me that day and have tried hard to live up to his ideals.

A ticket collector, calling loudly, 'Tickets please' brought me back to earth on my journey to 'civvy street' and to the realities of the present rather than the dreams of the unknown distant future.

After over six years of war, my ideas were somewhat confused to say the least. It took some time to come to terms with freedom. Throughout my service career I had been conditioned to obey orders and not to think too much for myself. My life was outside my control when I was drafted to the Russian convoys. There was no purpose in saying, or even thinking, I did not want to go. The order was given – I obeyed, and accepted the consequences. Now, at last, I was free and the challenge of the future was both exhilarating and alarming.

My ambition was to become a full-time artist and the obvious way in which I could resume my career was to return to the art college for extra tuition and a refresher course. I enrolled, using my gratuity to cover the cost of tuition, materials and living.

Times had changed the college. Most of the familiar faces among the staff had disappeared but it was wonderful to be back in familiar surroundings, with the attendant smells that I associated with the classrooms. The college helped to save my sanity and bring me back to reality.

There was a different atmosphere in the classrooms from the carefree days of pre-war. Many of the students were ex-servicemen from all spheres and ranks of the armed forces. We had all lost five or six years of our lives and were anxious to make up for lost time. There was an extra degree of earnestness in our work because we all realised that shortly we would have to start work for a living and try to commence or resume our careers.

Whilst in the services we had enjoyed an income and a degree of independence which had not been possible as young students straight from school. It was not easy to settle to student routines again but the adjustments had to be made. I soon began to feel a thrill when I picked up a brush and started to paint and before long I was looking forward to attending college each day.

At the end of the year I knew that I had to leave and start to make a living. As much as I dearly wanted to spend my time painting in water-colours, I had to acknowledge that it was very unlikely that I would be able to make a living that way. After the war years, very few people had any money to spend on luxuries such as paintings. They were busy rebuilding their lives and homes and any spare money was spent on necessities which, during the war, were either unobtainable or in short supply. Clothes, for example, were beginning to brighten up and become fashionable again, after years of coupons and utility quality. Holidays could be contemplated now that travelling restrictions had been removed. There were a hundred and one things people wanted to buy before considering the purchase of an original oil painting or water-colour by an unknown artist.

It was wonderful to be able to walk along the River Soar with my sketch book, after all the turmoil of war.

I realised this, and decided that I must seek employment in commercial art. I worked hard in preparing a portfolio of my work, which demonstrated the versatility of my artistic abilities. Everything was neatly finished and well presented, as I was anxious that the pride I had in my work would be evident to any prospective employer. My portfolio completed, I started to look for work. I made a list of possible employers, then visited their offices. Early in my travels I met the manager of a very large commercial art studio. He was obviously a busy man, no doubt rather tired of having starry-eyed art students knocking on his door asking for work. I was greeted with courtesy and invited to open my portfolio.

Fortunately my hours of preparation were rewarded, as his attention was attracted to some of my drawings, and it was not long before he had seen them all and offered me a job.

It was a very large studio and my first weeks were spent in having a few days in each department. I went through the market research, lettering, reproduction, drafting and illuminating departments and then had a few days in the library. This was the most fascinating of them all. There were files and cabinets full of drawings, notes, prints and photographs on every conceivable subject. They were all there for reference so that whatever was required by a customer could be reproduced with complete authenticity as to period, style and colour.

If, for instance, the background to an advertisement had to be a Victorian railway station, then within the library could be found references to show the style of barrows in use at the time, the type of seats on the platform and the colour of choco-

My first holiday after the war.
On the Broads 1947

late machines. Then there were the signs indicating waiting rooms, booking offices and the like to be considered, as well as the shape of the pelmets decorating the edges of platform roofs. Every effort was made to ensure that the facts were right before the design was shown to a customer.

The director had some advanced ideas, among which I most enjoyed the way he got a number of the staff together to thresh out a problem. He might call some of us into his room and then present us with a request he had received from a particular company. Perhaps it would be for a label for a tin of condensed milk. He would ask for ideas and suggestions would begin to flow, each sparking off another until he felt he had a really good basis on which to work. In this instance the design might be a happy cow, with tail in the air, jauntily running through a pasture full of buttercups, under a bright blue sky.

One of the artists was sent off to produce the label and when this was finished, if the director was not satisfied, we were all called in and he would say, 'Gentlemen, I am sure we can do better than this', and we all started tossing ideas round again. In this way, he eventually achieved the best possible results from our combined creative talents.

Much of my time with this company was spent on window dressing. After years of austerity and restrictions, outside influences from Scandinavia and America were beginning to affect the range of goods for sale in our shops. Trade, especially in fabrics and fashionable clothes, was increasing quickly. For the first time in their lives, potential customers had money in their pockets, which they were free to spend without having to worry about coupons. Shopkeepers were anxious to get their share of trade and were prepared to employ professional window dressers in order to do so.

At first I was given some of the small jobs to do. These included display cards, such as a painting or drawing of a man wearing a particular style of coat, suit, trousers or jacket. Often a small piece of cloth was pinned to the card, to indicate to a window-shopper what was in stock that could be used for making the garment.

The use of plastic for display units and stands was still in its infancy. It often fell to me in those early days, not only to design the units, but also to make them. There were very few which could be bought ready made, as manufacturers had been working on essential war requirements and only slowly were they able to adjust to peace-time needs.

Eventually I found myself responsible for the visual backgrounds, which was much more challenging and interesting. Sometimes these were made from gigantic enlarged photographs. For one I used a street scene on a wet day as the background for a display of raincoats. The people had their umbrellas up, some were scurrying along, leaning forward, trying to fend off the driving rain. For this display I was awarded a prize.

Usually the background was drawn and painted. Hardboard was not obtainable for window displays and I had to resort to the use of thick cardboard nailed on to wooden battens for my panels. Wallpaper was stuck over the cardboard to give a better surface for the final painting.

There was no plastic paint at the time. The only material that could be used, other than gloss paint, was the old fashioned distemper. Few colours were manufactured but I discovered that I could increase the range by mixing poster paints into the distemper.

With these very basic materials, I was able to get some very striking effects, as the pictures were on a grand scale. When designing the background I had to imagine what it would look like from the front of the window and even from across the other side of the road.

Overseas holidays were just beginning to be advertised and there was an interest in clothes suitable for wearing abroad. For one display I borrowed a model aircraft for the centre, and painted a background consisting of panels depicting the Greek Islands with the blue Mediterranean, and the Swiss Alps with their wooden chalets and colourful flowers.

Other backgrounds which I did included London scenes, landscapes, seascapes and lakes. Some of these I could do from my own knowledge, but for most I found the library invaluable to ensure the authenticity of what I was doing.

The old mill at Blickling

64

The business became part of a large group and a re-organisation followed. I found myself out of work and had to start looking for something else at which to make a living. There were no job centres to help and advise and at first I did not know what to do.

I had, for some time, been interested in murals or wall paintings and had studied work done by some of the artists who were well-known in this field. It occurred to me that I might be able to get some work in this way, although there were no contemporary murals in my area that I could find to study.

Nevertheless, I prepared some designs, both in sketches and water-colour, to make up a portfolio to show to potential customers. My first target was the large building contractors. As there was no such thing as the 'yellow pages' I had to prepare a list of possible companies from advertisements in the local papers, and from street and trade directories in the library.

I did not have a very encouraging start, to knocking on doors. Most of the managers said that they were very busy and could only spare a few minutes to look at my portfolio. Then I was shown the door with a courteous 'I'll call you if anything comes up.'

This went on for several days, until one of the builders I had seen earlier, telephoned and invited me back for further discussions. At the time all building work was controlled by licence, to make sure that as much effort and materials as possible was used in building houses and repairing damage caused by the war. The manager explained that he was beginning to get contracts for milk bars, which were becoming popular. His difficulty was that he was only permitted to use roughcast on the walls. This was perfectly satisfactory from the builder's point of view, as it was tough and durable and added strength to the walls. Of course, it did not give an appealing interior finish to customers while they sat drinking their milk shakes or expresso coffee.

Following my first visit, he had realised that murals on the walls would brighten the interior, while at the same time giving each bar a character of its own. He had discussed the idea with the proprietor in Hinkley, who was to have a milk bar called 'The Neptune Rooms' constructed and he had shown interest. I was therefore asked to produce designs for the walls.

I found this new challenge stimulating and within a few days my designs had been accepted and I started work on the murals. On one wall I painted King Neptune, with a big fat tummy, a seaweed skirt, greeny-yellow seaweed hair surmounted by a crown, and sitting on a rum barrel holding a trident. At his feet were pools of water in a rocky shore. On another wall I painted fishes in the sea as if they were swimming in an aquarium.

For this work I used ordinary undercoat paint for the overall background colour and then gloss for the remainder. Again, I

Mural of the Swiss Alps

was able to mix any colour from the base colours which were available.

This particular bar was in a cellar and when it had suitable lighting the murals were quite striking. The customer was delighted with the result and the builder offered me a full-time job with his company.

When there was a possibility of incorporating a mural into any contract, the builder took me to meet the customer and hinted that I was a technician whom he employed at great expense. In fact, I was only paid modestly but was glad to have employment at almost any price.

Another cellar that I worked on had imitation windows painted on the walls. These were complete with leaded lights opening into the room, with curtains and window boxes. On a panel of wood I painted scenes from the Swiss Alps at each of the windows. I was also involved in decorating bars in public houses. In 'The Highwayman' a wall was made to look as a bar would have done in the 17th century, complete with wooden beams across the ceiling. Near a door I painted some keys, apparently hanging on a piece of string from a nail. For added effect I knocked a nail into the wall and was often amused to see people try to take the keys off it, as they thought they also were real.

The idea caught the imagination of other customers and I was frequently employed in painting murals on the walls of factory canteens. During the war, these had become very drab and now an effort was being made to refurbish them and brighten them up. Occasionally, I was given a free hand to do as I pleased. When this happened, I usually produced scenes of the seaside, with lobster pots, boats, muddy creeks and rotting posts with a few sea birds flying over.

The work lasted for a few years until the family decided to dissolve the business and once again I was unemployed. During this period I had begun to enjoy a reasonable standard of living and it came as a bit of a blow to be thrown back on my own resources, looking for work again.

By this time, building regulations had been relaxed, new materials were becoming available and styles of interior decorating, too, were changing. I could not find another full-time job and was forced to undertake casual and part-time work.

While I had been painting murals I had kept an interest in what the other workers were doing. I had picked up some knowledge of interior decorating, enabling me to undertake work of that nature. I explored my local neighbourhood and managed to find some household decorating jobs. I was so desperate to earn some money that I tackled everything I was offered. Sometimes, if I was lucky, I could persuade the person who was employing me to have a small mural at an extra cost. Strangely, the most popular place for a mural was on bathroom walls.

One day, while scanning the local paper, I saw an advertisement for insurance agents. I applied and got the job, finding myself with a 'book' and a round to do. As I did not have a car I used my bicycle or walked, as I traversed the streets collecting weekly, fortnightly or monthly contributions on insurance policies. As this did not take many hours each day it could be fitted in with other part-time work.

Occasionally I still received commissions for large murals in commercial buildings and also for window dressing displays. If I had very little else to do I went to building sites to see if there was any casual help needed. I found Saturday morning was

often a good time as there were odd jobs that had to be done before the weekend. I would find myself cleaning out the cement mixer, a wet messy job that nobody liked to do, but I was glad to earn the ten shillings I was given for it.

There was an added bonus, as when I got to know the site foremen, I managed to 'acquire' off-cuts of hardboard and partly used cans of plastic emulsion paint which were being thrown away. The paint was ideal for dressing the hardboard before I used it for oil paintings.

Unexpectedly one day I received an approach from a national oil company who were seeking someone with experience of commercial art to work in their advertising and sales promotion department. Although this was the job I was offered and accepted, for all the time that I worked for them I was a 'technical oil representative'.

The world of big business was completely new to me but I was soon enjoying the work, especially as I was given a company car which I could use at the weekend for private purposes. By this time I was married and had a son and a daughter and the car enabled me to take the family out into the countryside.

I became responsible for drawing diagrams and illustrations for the company brochures. This would sometimes mean visiting a car factory to look at cutaway engines to produce sketches of how lubricating oils reduced the wear and tear of moving parts. There was considerable interest in petrol additives, and one brochure I produced indicated why they were effective and how they functioned. The secret was that the additives helped to maintain a film of oil on the metal and thus prevent the friction and wear caused by direct metal to metal contact.

Sometimes there would be a panic, when market research showed that a competitor had a larger share of the market than we had for a certain product. On one occasion it was the sale of oil on the forecourts of garages which had declined. I was sent out to try to find the reason and after speaking to about fifty forecourt attendants, realised that it was simply due to the shape of the can. Most of the attendants did not bother with brand names, they just picked up the can which was most easy to handle and open. After discovering this, I had to redesign a new can which the company has continued to use.

This might seem trivial but it illustrates the need for everything to be designed. Thought has to be given to all the things we use, they do not just happen. Somebody has to design and manufacture them.

The company had an annual conference when all the staff, from the managing director to the newest recruit, gathered in an hotel. Large hotels at seaside resorts such as Scarborough, Brighton and Blackpool could be relatively cheaply hired out of season and one of them would be the venue. I met many of the representatives and was particularly pleased when I got to

Morning light at Pin Mill

69

know Sam, who was a senior representative working in Norfolk, as my ambition was to move there some day. Over the next year or two I got to know him well.

The managing director had a very high regard for Sam, and when he became ill was anxious to help in any way possible. The problem was caused when Sam developed angina and the company doctor would not allow him to drive while at work. The only way, therefore, to retain his services was to provide him with a driver. Fortunately Sam indicated that he would like me to do it. The managing director agreed and I was sent to Norfolk as a 'technical oil representative', although in reality I spent most of my time acting as a chauffeur for Sam. Thus the company was prepared to pay for me to move to Norfolk which I was very pleased to do.

Finding a house proved difficult. Sam lived near Fakenham, so I wanted to be fairly close to him but I also wanted to be near the north Norfolk coast. I sold my house in Oadby without difficulty and thought that I had bought a house in North Walsham until it came time to sign contracts, when the seller decided to change her mind and withdrew the property from the market.

This put me in a desperate position. Frantically I searched villages along the coast for an old house but found nothing suitable. Then one day, as I was passing through North Walsham, I called at an estate agent and was offered a bungalow in Aylsham. 'Where's Aylsham?' I asked and he quickly explained.

All the time that I had been living in Leicestershire I had continued to paint, both in oils and water-colours, whenever I could find the time. For the first year or two, after being demobbed, I painted almost entirely in the countryside in the area where I lived, and which was within cycling distance.

It was while I was doing some window dressing for his company that I met Stan Witcher. He was interested in my work as an artist and enquired if I had any paintings of the north Norfolk coast as he had a cottage there and would like to buy a painting of the area.

When I told him that I was new to the district, he said, 'Then you must come and stay with me one weekend at my cottage at Blakeney'. It was early spring and although it was overcast and raining heavily I remember my first glimpse of Morston church. Immediately, I was enchanted with it and the unspoilt little village. I had the feeling that this was where I wanted to paint and I knew I would have to return there again after the weekend.

Stan showed me around Blakeney, which still retained its pre-war charm and was much as it had been for the past fifty years. Few houses had been turned into weekend cottages and most of the buildings which have now been converted were still being used for their original purpose, or lay unused and empty.

Stan introduced me to the White Horse where I met Stratton Long, his brother Walter and his mother, who served in the bar wearing solid gold earrings, which enhanced the strong features of her face. Then we went further down the village to the King's Arms where he introduced me to other local characters. I was already beginning to feel at home as we strolled along to talk to someone working on a boat in the yard adjacent to the pub. As we stopped for a chat, I thought how handy it was to be able to pop next door for a drink when work in the boatyard had created a thirst.

We were so enthralled looking at what had to be done to restore the boat that we did not notice a holiday maker looking at us. He wanted to know what we were doing and I explained as best I could from the knowledge gained in the previous ten minutes. Satisfied, he put his hand in his pocket, gave me some money for a drink, and left me standing dumbfounded that I had already been mistaken for a native.

'. . . he put his hand into his pocket . . '

A little further along Stan and I had 'lunch' at a fish and chip

shop, where the most delicious fish and chips could be bought for a few pennies.

Stan sensed that I had fallen in love with the area and generously let me have the cottage for a week later in the summer. I was married by then, and my understanding and long-suffering wife sat for hours alongside the muddy creeks while I painted and sketched. I was fascinated by the sun glistening on the wet mud and by the boats leaning at crazy angles when the tide ebbed, and the thousand and one other things that could be found in and around the fishing villages of this coast.

One day, as I was painting, the landlord of the King's Arms happened to come past, looked over my shoulder and must have liked what he saw, as he invited me to take it into his pub and said he would hang it up for sale. I could not mount or frame it but nevertheless, it was sold before I had to go home. In Leicestershire I was selling a few pictures due to the annual exhibitions of the Leicester Society of Arts, and the Leicester Sketch Club. Dan introduced me to both events, which were well established organisations and well attended. At the private viewing I was actually lucky enough to sell one out of the three paintings I was allowed to hang.

When the exhibitions opened to the public, in the early days I used to enjoy mingling with the crowd and eavesdrop on their remarks about the various pictures. It was a tremendous thrill to see a red spot on my paintings as the small amount of money they fetched was badly needed to buy more paper and paints and, of course, I realised that I would gradually become known if my paintings were sold.

At various times, when I had only part-time employment, I could spend more time painting. When I was acting as an insurance agent for instance, I could often complete my round soon enough to fit some painting in during the afternoon.

By the early 1960's I was becoming well enough known for people to come to my house to buy paintings. This was very encouraging and reinforced my resolve to ultimately become a full-time artist.

My growing reputation was further enhanced by a commission to produce a painting for a calendar for the local paper, the *Leicester Mercury*. This was followed by a similar commission for the Lockheed company, and also for illustrations for a limited edition of a leather-bound desk diary.

But all the time, I felt I was being drawn back to Blakeney. The real difficulty was that I had no transport of my own and the journey was nearly impossible by public transport. Somehow I discovered that there was a bus going from Leicester to the convalescent hospital at Overstrand on some Sundays, and I managed to do a few trips on it.

It dropped me off on the Kelling road near Holt and I walked the three miles or so to the village, did one painting and some sketching and walked back to catch the bus on its return journey. I found that I could sell my paintings in the King's Arms and this was the start of a very happy friendship with the landlord that lasted for many years.

After each painting expedition I went home, finished off the painting I had worked on, then did a few more from the sketches I had made. They then had to be mounted and framed ready for sale.

I could not do many as I had to carry them from the bus, drop them in at the King's Arms, then set off to paint on the coast line. Fortunately, I did not have much material to carry and all that I had fitted easily into a modest haversack.

As soon as I could afford it I decided to buy a little car to make the journey less arduous and so that my wife could come with me. The opportunity arose when an insurance policy for £50 matured. I managed to find an Austin Ruby for sale at just this amount. It needed new tyres, but this was not a great problem or expense as I bought a set from a dump for £1. These were heavy duty tyres used on motor bicycles which also fitted the car. Then I gave the body, and the spiked wheels a coat of paint and it was ready for the road. It enabled me to have longer days painting during the summer, and also with my wife and young children to explore more of Norfolk. We used it to tour the Broads as well as the coastal villages.

Stan continued to let me have his cottage. The trips to Blakeney, to the King's Arms to see Gus, became more regular, and still I could sell all the pictures I produced. At the end of many a wonderful day Jo and I have chugged back to Leicestershire in our little Austin Ruby at a sedate 30 miles per hour, with a prayer that it would surmount all the hills on the way. Eventually it was replaced by the oil company's car.

Winter in the Dales

CHAPTER 6

Part-time Artist

The estate agent told me that Aylsham was about five miles from North Walsham, and that he could easily arrange for me to view the property. The bungalow that I was offered was on a small estate just on the outskirts of town. It was far from complete but had come on the market again as the original buyer had decided not to proceed with the purchase.

The following morning I picked up a key and went to look at it. First impressions were very deceptive. There were no hard roads or paths, but plenty of wet, soft, sticky mud. I picked the cleanest approach I could find to the bungalow but I need not have bothered for inside everything was in chaos with dust everywhere. In fact, only the shell had been completed so I was left to imagine what it would be like when walls were plastered, doors, cupboards and kitchen fitted, and the interior decorated.

I stood looking out on to the rutted mud which was to be my back garden and wondered how I could commit my wife and two young children to come and live there. There was no way that Jo could get over to see it in the next few days so I had the unenviable task of making the decision on whether or not to buy the property. In the end, I felt that I was left with no option, as we desperately needed somewhere to live and there was unlikely to be anywhere else available. I just had to accept it. When I returned the key and told the agent I was willing to buy, I thought that this would provide the family with a roof over its head 'for the time being'. In the event, that bungalow is still our home, although over the years we have made alterations and extensions to suit our needs.

Our house in Leicester had been sold and when we moved to Aylsham, the bungalow was still unfinished. There was still no path, the floor tiles had not been laid and water was only available from an outside tap. Nick, my six-year-old son, had a pet rabbit which escaped while the furniture was being unloaded. Our first introduction to the estate, therefore, was to search for the rabbit through the mud, amongst all the paraphernalia of the builder's equipment and supplies. Thankfully we found it and were able to return to the bungalow and start to settle in.

74

After a few weeks, we began to feel that the worst was over. The builder had fully completed all the interior work and we had good paths to walk on. The children became accustomed to their changed surroundings and began to make new friends. Nick noticed the difference between Leicestershire and Norfolk very acutely to begin with. He came home after his first day at school with wonderment in his eyes and exclaimed, 'we have a real fire in our classroom', which must have contrasted sharply with the centrally heated classroom to which he had become accustomed.

Within a few months Jo and I had started to become involved with local affairs and gradually joined in more and more activities. It was not long before we realised that rather than being our home for 'the time being' it was likely to remain so for many years to come.

In the meantime, I was working with Sam, driving him around Norfolk to visit his customers and pick up orders and get to know them against the time when I would eventually take over from him. Many of his customers were farmers, some of whom had already bought paintings from me. On many occasions when we visited a farmer, he would look at me quizically with an expression of, 'Haven't I seen you somewhere before?' on his face. Most found it difficult to reconcile that this young oil representative was a part-time artist but they

Burnham Overy mill

75

The last load

were very generous and as I got to know them better, would
occasionally combine an order for a few thousand gallons of
diesel with the sale of a water-colour.

At first sight, my position with the company seemed ideal,
with a company car, a pension fund and private medical treat-
ment. The snag was that my salary was based entirely on commission. Each month an advance payment was made and at the
end an adjustment, based on sales, was made before receipt of
the next advance. I found this system most difficult, as with a
young family and mortgage it seemed to be a rather hand-to-
mouth existence but in effect, it was probably good preparation for the years ahead.

I had been working in Norfolk for less than two years when
unfortunately Sam died. Now I was on my own and I suppose I
should have accepted the challenge with open arms but my
heart was in painting and I did not want to spend the rest of my
life selling oil. The director of the company was understanding
and encouraging when I told him that I intended to resign. He
had already purchased some of my paintings and therefore
realised that I wanted to become a professional artist. He
appreciated the risk I was taking and very generously offered
to keep my job open for 12 months should I wish to return to
the company. For that period the area was shared between two
other representatives from adjoining areas.

Whether or not to stay with the oil company was an
agonising decision, but it was made much easier when I

received an offer from a gallery in Holt to buy one of my pictures each week. This was not sufficient to give me a living but it was a tremendous help in assessing what I was going to do. If I left the company, I would lose my car, knowing full well that I would not be able to buy one and would have to go back to a bicycle. I would lose my monthly salary, my pension and private medical insurance.

On the other hand, I must earn enough money to pay living expenses and the mortgage, without any guarantee that my paintings would continue to sell. I was very fortunate to have the support of my wife who had confidence that I would succeed and was prepared to put up with any hardship as a consequence of my decision. Also, after leaving the services I had often found it necessary to fall back on my own resources to make a living. This had built my self-confidence, therefore I believed in myself and felt sure that I had the enthusiasm, talent and energy to succeed.

There was just one thing that worried me tremendously. I could see that my future livelihood depended on the use of my left hand with which I sketched and painted. Stories of dancers insuring their legs and pianists insuring their hands came into my mind. Forthwith I took out a personal liability insurance on my hand. It cost only a few pence but it was comforting to have, as I was guaranteed several weeks pay should I become unable to paint through an accident.

Although I had resigned from the oil company and had decided to become a professional artist, I was still not sure that my painting alone would bring in enough money to meet my family commitments. When the milkman knocked on the door for his money, I knew it would be useless to say, 'sorry, but there is no money as I have not been creative this week'.

One day, I met a young builder in Aylsham market place and told him of my concern and hope that I could get a little part-time work somewhere. He was quiet for a little while, then said he could use my services as a driver on two mornings each week. The problem was that he had some workers who were unable to drive and so, in order to keep them supplied with materials, another driver had to be taken from his work on the site to drive the van.

It was agreed that I would work for him on a casual basis. Most days when I arrived for work I would find a list of things needed for the day. This I took to the wholesalers, who were mostly in Norwich, then went on my rounds delivering a door here, a window there or some pipes somewhere else. Then if anything else was required I went to fetch it. Sometimes it was just a question of taking the non-drivers to their respective building sites.

Their needs were many and various. It could be a load of cement, or long lengths of timber either fastened to the roof or sticking out beyond the back of the van. My work on the building sites in Leicestershire had given me some good grounding. Carrying bags of cement up a long garden path I could easily take in my stride. If a little help was needed to dig out some foundations, or a hole for a cesspit, I was quite willing to oblige.

The vehicle I drove was an old white van, which I soon named the 'laughing cow'. This was because I remembered the story of a U-boat commander who had a painting of a smiling cow with a bell round its neck, romping through a green meadow, on the conning-tower of his submarine. I believe he got the idea from a condensed milk tin, and the van reminded me of a tin on wheels, hence the name with which I christened it.

One day in the depth of winter, when the roads were icy, I was driving a group of workers home in the evening, when smoke began to appear from behind the dash-board. The brakes were none too good, and as I tried to stop, the van skidded from one side of the road to the other. As I struggled with the van, the man in the passenger seat wrenched the wires out and this prevented the fumes from developing into a full-blown fire. Miraculously, the good old 'laughing cow' carried on as if nothing had happened.

Eventually, when it became unroadworthy, I was given the task of dumping it in a pit. With one of the builders I took it as near to the edge as possible and we gently pushed it over. It rolled over and bumped against the side of the quarry side but somehow landed upright and we could hear, in spite of all, the engine was still running. She just did not want to die.

My painting was somewhat restricted by not having a car. I travelled as far as I could round the district on my bicycle. I did not lack subjects but longed to get back to the coast which, although only 9 or 10 miles away, was difficult to visit in the limited time at my disposal.

I spent many happy hours walking the lanes of Aylsham. In the early morning if I was not working, I took my labrador bitch Sheba for a walk. Often I walked past the Carmen brothers' farm. the very first time that one of them spoke to me he said, 'Hello, old partner' which puzzled me at the time, as I wondered how he knew my name, not realising that it was a common form of address in Norfolk.

As I did not have a studio in those early days, I painted in the bungalow. My favourite place was at the kitchen sink. If I propped my board up against the taps, it was at a very convenient height for working and my paints could be put on the draining board. For most of the day the light was very good but in summer and during winter afternoons, it became very difficult to paint near the west facing window. It was also, of course, extremely difficult for domestic reasons to be working away for hours and so restricting use of the sink.

After a little searching around, I managed to rent a single room in an empty cottage. There was no furniture so I went to the local market and bought an old chest of drawers and a chair

The end of the 'laughing cow'

for a few shillings. This was all I needed and was the only furnishing I had during the time I occupied this 'studio'.

There was no way of providing heat. In the summer this mattered very little but in the winter I spent many cold days there, wrapped up in several layers of sweaters. Because there was no heat the walls were damp and mildew growth covered the outside walls and part of the ceiling. The cold damp atmosphere did not deter me from spending as much time as I could working there.

When the weather was suitable, I painted outside, direct from nature but I also made numerous sketches which could be worked at when bad weather drove me indoors.

With the departure of the 'laughing cow', I was able to devote more time to painting and was just getting used to a routine of painting almost every day, when there was a severe outbreak of influenza in Aylsham. The postmaster, who had bought some of my paintings, knew that I was still looking for some part-time work. One day when I went into the post office to buy some stamps, he asked me if I would be interested in helping out as a postman for two weeks because so many of his staff were sick. He indicated that it would only be for a few hours each morning and then I would have the rest of the day for painting.

I agreed that it was just what I wanted and then enquired what time I would have to start work. To my amazement he said 5.00 a.m. but this was no great hardship as I was accustomed to early rising.

The first day I was shown how to sort the mail as conveniently as possible for delivery. One of the regular staff accompanied me on my round, after that I was left to my own devices. The mail bag, full of letters and small packages, weighed heavily round my neck at the start of the round. By walking briskly I could finish quickly but in the process, over the first two weeks, I lost 7lb in weight which was beneficial to my waist line.

At the end of my prescribed period some of the staff were still sick and I was asked to continue 'for the time being'. Eventually, by the time the epidemic was over, and some staff had been on holiday, my postman days lasted for nine months.

I got to know where all the letter boxes were, no matter how cunningly they were hidden, whether to the side, bottom or top of a door, round a corner or behind some plants growing on the house wall. The worst were those at the bottom rail of a door, as when I stooped down to put the mail through, my bag swung off my shoulder, and if I happened to be wearing a cape because it was raining, the bag and cape became entangled. Often I thought that designers of letter boxes should be made to deliver letters through them, then they would soon learn to think again about where they should be positioned.

Some of the letter boxes were on the bottom rail

Gates I found to be highly individual. Some needed pushing down to unlatch, others needed lifting up. Some swung open of their own accord while others had to be manhandled. There was also the ever present threat from the pet dog. Most of them seemed to have an instinctive hate of postmen and I quickly got to know the households who kept a dog, and how to avoid it when necessary.

There was one particularly vicious dog, which rushed to the door, barking loudly as I approached down the garden path. I suppose I was rather slow in getting the letters through the box and a tug of war developed as the dog snatched at the correspondence, reducing it to mutilated pieces of paper. I realised afterwards that the regular postman pushed the letters through the box with alacrity and the dog just picked them up off the mat.

My efforts continued for a few days, until the irate householder accosted me, complaining about the state of his post. I quickly pointed out that if he kept his vicious dog under control, all would be well. From that time, I could hear the animal barking faintly, so he must have been shut in one of the rooms and normal deliveries were resumed.

Sometimes when I had a package to deliver, it was necessary to knock on the door. One morning in late summer, I was delivering a package and had to go along the side of the house past the kitchen window to get to the back door, as nobody appeared to use the front door. As I passed the window, I glanced in and there, standing at the cooker frying eggs and

80

Wildfowl. Misty morning on the Broads

bacon, was the lady of the house, stark naked. Fortunately, she had her back to me and I crept backwards, fearing that at any moment she would turn and see me.

Having regained my ground, I knocked loudly on the front door an after a short while there was a clatter of bolts being undone and the door was opened by a charming young housewife suitably clad in a red dressing gown, completely oblivious of the fact that I had seen her through the kitchen window.

Whilst working as a postman, I had also been instructing at an evening class in Aylsham. On two nights each week there was a full house and it was a great success. It seems that Mr. Asquith, the then headmaster of nearby Cawston College, had heard of the classes and, as a result, contacted me and asked if I would be prepared to take on some part-time teaching at the college.

'. . . standing at the cooker
frying bacon and eggs

The Ouse Washes at Welney

His problem was that art was being taught by a science master, who could only spend a few hours on the subject and to make matters worse, he intended to retire in the near future. I was asked to go there for two hours in the morning on three days a week. This did not seem to interfere unduly with my painting, and as I enjoyed teaching, I readily agreed to take up the position. I became engrossed in the work and for several years spent some happy days at the college.

I was given complete control of the art curriculum, leaving me to buy any materials that were required by the boys. Some of the pupils were brilliant in many subjects and some, as I had been, were less accomplished on the academic side. I got a tremendous thrill from helping them all to develop their talents, and seeing their work progress and improve as the days went by. At the end of the first year, 17 of my pupils were entered for 'O' level art and 16 of them gained passes. Such success was very rewarding for me, as well as the pupils, and gave me considerable encouragement for the terms ahead.

The integration of art with history added a new dimension to my classes. Annually there was a parents day, for which displays were specially prepared. I realised that with the long history of the Norfolk people there were some fruitful fields to explore. Typical of these was the panorama of a Viking village which the boys made.

Soon after my arrival at the college, I had started classes in modelling and sculpture in clay. Although there was no kiln, if the models were left in a drying room for a few weeks, they became firm enough to handle and paint. Firstly, model huts, thatched with straw and village figures, were made from clay.

Then a large model of a Viking ship, complete with oars, was put together. To authenticate everything we made, the pupils had to refer to their history books, or perhaps to the library.

In arranging the model village on a table, my experience in commercial art and window display proved invaluable. As a background to the panorama, the lads painted a typical coastal scene, which had probably changed very little over the past centuries. The end result was so striking that I am sure that many of the parents were surprised at the talent their sons had shown by producing the display. From my point of view it was most gratifying to find that given a lead, together with some help and encouragement, unexpected enthusiasm and co-operation can be obtained from the college pupils.

Throughout the seven years that I taught at Cawston, I tried to maintain a wide curriculum in art, to make sure that every-one was catered for and particular aptitudes were developed. My own preference was for water-colour painting and inevit-ably more time was devoted to that than to other types of art. The class members spent much of their time on sketching and painting still life indoors, but whenever the weather was suit-able I took them into the surrounding gardens and country-side.

Gradually, the success of the college in 'O' and 'A' level examination results was recognised by complimentary comments received from the Board of Examiners. Several of the pupils produced acceptable paintings which parents wisely and proudly framed. Today when I visit their homes, I still find examples hanging on the walls of both their parents' and their own homes.

The wider implications of my teaching are, I believe, also evident in my pupils' attitude to art and the countryside. Since the college was situated in the heart of rural Norfolk, many of them came from the farming community, and with the passage of years they are now farming themselves. Although they had no pretensions to becoming artists — and I suspect have not put a paint-brush to paper since leaving college — when I meet them, I feel that their enjoyment of the countryside has been enhanced by having been taught to look at colours and composition. In a changing countryside, when more emphasis is now being put on conservation, I believe that when tree and hedge planting is being planned, to be able to look at the view through an artist's eye is a tremendous help towards deciding just what to do.

Over the years at Cawston, I found that I was spending more and more time at the college. I loved teaching and wanted to help each boy as much as I possibly could. I became engrossed in trying to develop talent and found that frequently I stayed an extra hour to give some individual tuition. This often led to be being asked to stay for lunch and, enjoyable as it was, the more time I spent at the college, the less I had available for painting.

After seven happy years I felt I had to decide whether to continue teaching or to become a professional artist. I had, by that time, built up a sufficient clientele to pursue my life's ambition and, therefore, reluctantly resigned from the college staff. It was an amicable but somewhat sad parting, as I left with very mixed feelings, wanting to carry on teaching yet knowing that the break had to be made.

On the day I left, the boys sprung a surprise on me. They collected together to buy a pair of cut-glass brandy glasses, and used their art to good effect. When I went into the classroom for the last time, the walls were festooned with sketches and paintings, depicting me taking part in various sporting activities. They had realised that I had never been very good at any sport and had chosen to portray some of my inept attempts at cricket and rugby as topics to ridicule.

It was a moving farewell but I still see many of my old pupils from time to time, and am especially proud when I see the work of some of the professional artists who were my former pupils.

High and dry at Brancaster Staithe

CHAPTER 7

Demonstrations and Exhibitions

Soon after I moved to Aylsham I was invited to join Rotary and, as is customary for new members, I was asked to give a short talk. In the time available I could only make some comments on the Old English style of water-colours, in which medium I now painted, as I had virtually given up painting in oils.

Following this, I was asked to talk at a number of Women's Institute meetings and found myself increasingly in demand. After a while, I thought I could make the evenings more entertaining if, instead of just talking about painting, I actually demonstrated how I did it. To do this I had to devise a way which allowed the audience to see as much of my working methods as possible, and to be able to watch the picture grow.

When working out of doors, I often stand up, balancing my board on my knee as I like to be able to move it around when applying washes. During my talks I changed my style a little and worked with the board at least at shoulder level. With my paints on a card table, I was then able to move the board around and talk as I demonstrated my technique. All I had to do in preparation was to make a sketch ready for painting, exactly as I would in my studio or out in the countryside.

One local report described a talk thus:

> 'Using a water-colour board on which was drawn Morston Bridge, he produced his equipment. This consisted of an old white dinner plate picked up in a jumble sale for 3d, which was his palette, a margarine tub which held his water, and a cardboard lid which held the plate at an angle. Then, with his most expensive item, a number 12 brush which cost £40, he started to paint.'
>
> *(Eastern Evening News)*

On another occasion I was invited to give a demonstration at the Fakenham Festival. I felt very honoured to do so, as such nationally known figures such as Humphrey Littleton and David Jacobs also took part in the programme.

The evening was very well received and, again, I quote from a local press report of the event:

> 'Swishing jokes and tips to a packed audience as liberally as he used his paint, he left Rolf Harris a long way behind.

Ploughing horses

It was all a piece of fun he said, but his two works – both painted in an astonishing spell of 40 minutes – had amateur artists gasping.

They were clearly not masterpieces, but the basic skills and tricks of the trade were there all employed, not exactly in black and white, but for all to see.

The tender tones, the gentle flowing movements of the blended colours, and through it all a tremendous awareness of light and shadow dominate his work.

Skies are clearly a fascination for this Norfolk-based artist. And even in his so-called Rolf Harris specials there was a naturalness about the skies, so often missing in many landscapes.

A man who loves his work – perhaps the wrong word to use for his art – he proved a witty and down-to-earth speaker. Mixing funny stories with hints on the construction of paintings, the advantages of good tools, and certain grades of paper, he gave the impression that he could have gone on all night.'

(Dereham & Fakenham Times)

Over the years I have given demonstrations to innumerable meetings for many organisations, including charities which have used the evenings for fund raising. On such nights I often donated the picture for auction, and on each occasion it met a ready bidder. This was in spite of it being merely a coloured sketch, which really required several hours work in the studio to give it a final finish.

Also, I have spoken to numerous art groups and have followed these by arranging field visits, when I could give individual help to members. Later in the year I was often invited back to undertake the dubious privilege of judging their annual art exhibition.

I am not able to judge how effective these demonstrations were but I believe they increased the interest of many people in art and helped others to improve their technique and enjoyment in painting. But I do know of one case of over-reaction.

It occurred after a demonstration at an art club meeting. One man in the audience, who I believe was a police inspector, due to retire in the near future, became so convinced that painting was easy that he decided to have a try and make it his retirement hobby. He was sure that there was nothing to it and that he could soon produce some saleable pictures.

Next morning he went into town and purchased a range of the most expensive sable brushes, costing from £20 to £60 each at that time, colours in boxes and tubes, paper and board, costing well over a total of £200. Undaunted, he thought that this outlay would soon be recovered by the sale of a picture or two.

I was, of course, unaware of this until the following day when I had a very angry man on the 'phone complaining that I had given a totally wrong impression and had made painting look deceptively easy, when it was really very difficult. He explained that he had bought the best of equipment but when he sat down to paint, nothing flowed from his brush as it had from mine on the previous evening. He just could not achieve the look he wanted and was particularly irate about the skies, which he expected me to be able to put right over the 'phone.

I tried to explain that nothing comes without perseverance and hard work and that the only way to improve was to practice as much as he could.

Many members of audiences think that painting must be easy and will sometimes comment to my wife about how much I can accomplish in 40 minutes. Her reply is 'Not in 40 minutes, in 30 years and 40 minutes'. Few seem to realise that I spent years at college to learn my technique and that ever since I have been improving by continuous practice. Most people seem to think that art can be learned in six easy lessons or, in the case of the man mentioned above, one extremly difficult one.

With the growing interest which these activities generated, and the increasing number of clients buying my paintings, I felt the time had come to realise the dreams of all artists – to have a one-man exhibition. My resolve was encouraged by the suggestion of the manager of the Assembly House, Norwich, Mr. R. (Charles) Rounce that I should hold my exhibition there.

Originally built by Thomas Ivory in 1754, the Assembly House was restored after the Second World War by Harry

Sexton, who wanted it to be used and enjoyed by everyone, while maintaining its elegance and style. Now it is the home of numerous societies which regularly meet there. It has its own cinema and a restaurant which has been described as 'The best self-service establishment in England'. It also has two rooms which, for much of the year, are hired by artists and craftsmen to exhibit their work.

The larger of the two, is the Ivory Room, and this I hired for two weeks as I had been told that artists usually sell, on average, one picture each day. On the opening day, I sold all the pictures I had, much to Charles' astonishment and my delight. Although I faced 13 days ahead when I could do nothing, other than talk to visitors, I was naturally overjoyed. This was the start of a very happy relationship with the Assembly House, which still continues.

I find selling directly to my clientele deeply satisfying as I am then involved with them and get to know them in such a way that many have become friends. I have known some families long enough for the children, now grown up, to come to my exhibitions, and many a proud grandparent has purchased a painting for a newly-born grandchild.

Post mill at Ixworth

Frequently a purchaser will discuss a painting he has bought,

pointing out particular points of interest and recounting memories which the scene invokes. It deepens my feeling for the area and when I return, it has an even greater significance than on earlier visits.

Selling through a gallery is a much more detached arrangement. The paintings are delivered, hung, and — hopefully — sold, but the artist does not usually meet the client and there is no rapport between them. Not all artists think like this but I like to sell direct, and most of my work is sold in this way.

On one occasion I was invited by a London gallery to discuss selling my work there. I suppose that I was flattered at being invited to do so by such an august and well-known establishment.

When I arrived, I was received in a room, where I sank ankle deep into the carpet and sat down in a silk upholstered chair, while coffee was poured from a silver service into the most delicate and exquisite china cups.

After a while we began to discuss what the gallery was offering. 'How much would you expect to sell my paintings for?' I asked. The reply indicated a price about double the price at which I was selling them. 'How much would you pay me?' I ventured to ask and was told a figure similar to the price at which I was selling in Norfolk. 'Why would I not get a greater share of the sale price?' I enquired. 'Well, we have a very expensive gallery to maintain' was the reply, 'and need a high profit margin. Of course, if your paintings become popular, the prices will increase and you will reap some of the benefit'.

It was not only the price aspect which concerned me, I was even more worried that the gallery insisted on exclusive rights to all my work during the period that I was under contract to them. This meant that sales at home would have to cease and I would no longer be able to have my Norwich exhibitions. Needless to say, I refused their offer and returned home a very disappointed man, as I had travelled up hoping that I was to be asked to supply a few paintings from time to time and that I would then have an established London outlet.

I gradually built up a considerable list of people to invite to my exhibitions, which for 17 years were held on an annual basis. They were always held in the spring and throughout the autumn and winter I tried to build up a supply of paintings just for that exhibition. In some years, by Christmas, I found that I had sold most of the autumn's work and then had to concentrate in the next month or two on replacing those intended for the exhibition. At one time, my framer used to keep all that I sent to him, to make sure that I did not sell them in the meantime.

My commercial training was very useful with arrangements such as mailing lists, invitations and cataloguing, pricing and finally, hanging. I realised that it was desirable to have a range of work on offer and I tried to vary the subjects to satisfy as

many tastes as possible and always had a range of sizes and prices to cater for all pockets.

After the first exhibition or two, I felt that I must try to give my regular clients some priority in being able to purchase, and held a preview the night before the public opening. This was very successful in that paintings were sold but some people were disappointed that since they could not get to the preview, they had little choice the next day, and those not receiving invitaions wondered why not.

I felt that I had to return to the usual arrangement with the doors opening at 10.30 a.m. on a Monday morning. At 10.00 o'clock a queue began to form, among which were some people who had travelled some distance and had stayed overnight in Norwich to make sure that they could be there on time.

When the doors opened, people came in, picked up a catalogue and then quietness fell over the room as everybody had a quick look round. This was followed by a loud buzz as my wife, a friend and I took names and put red spots on the paintings as they were sold. There was a frantically busy two hours before lunch, by which time, usually, most of the works for sale had been sold.

Then for the rest of the time there would be a steady flow of old friends who had called to see me. Perhaps they had just come to look around, or perhaps discuss a picture they wished to commission. It might be a specific request for a house, church, farm or a particular view, or it might just be a general enquiry for a picture of the Suffolk coast, or one of horses or birds. All were recorded and I would use my best endeavours to meet their requirements.

I must confess that some commissions are not executed for a very long time, usually because of commitments to other subjects. Some of my clients who became desperate to have a painting for a certain date − a birthday or anniversary for instance − got to know that the only way to generate delivery was to ring me a time or two until their order was committed to my 'panic' list. Once on this list, the work is given priority and usually the deadline is met, even if it means having to take the painting to the framer, wait while he frames it, then rush off to deliver it by car.

Over the years of my exhibitions, I got to know most of the visitors, even those who never bought a picture. But some were regular attenders who never spoke. I particularly remember one elderly lady who, for many years, never missed the first morning. As she came in she picked up a catalogue and proceeded to look at every painting, scrutinising it and examining every detail. This took about an hour when she would very carefully replace the catalogue on the pile and disappear from the room. I presumed she went to have a cup of coffee, for after a short time she returned and repeated the performance. Some visitors like to look at the paintings closely, others stand back, some spend a few minutes, others an hour or two. All

91

have different stances, some lean forward, others lean back.

The individual idiosyncracies were highlighted for me one year when another artist called Pipkin, who was living in Norfolk at that time, had an exhibition of his work in the Hobart Room. Earlier in his career he had been a cartoonist and throughout the duration of our exhibitions he did quick sketches of the visitors, and from time to time popped in and left them on the table in my room. Each bore a short cryptic note, such as 'Has she been in yet?' 'I think he is probably a Duke', or 'Norfolk farmer' or 'Bank manager'. With the facility of a good cartoonist he was able to pick out a recognisable feature of the face, dress or stance of the person and I had no difficulty in recognising his 'portraits'.

A visitor

CHAPTER 8

Norfolk Days

After leaving Cawston College, the need for a studio became of paramount importance. Neither the kitchen sink, nor a room in the bungalow was adequate for full-time working. The problem was solved by having a large wooden shed erected in my garden. This was not very big, but was sufficient to house some books and to provide space for a bench and chair. A large window with a northern aspect was ideal for working as the light which came through was exactly what I needed. This studio has been invaluable to me and I still do most of my work in it. The only modification over the years has been an adjustable drawing board to replace the piece of wood propped up against some books, and an extension to provide a small gallery where clients can view paintings for sale.

At last, I was now free to explore Norfolk and spend as much time as I wanted on the subjects which most interested me, which fortunately also seemed to be favoured by my clients.

I returned to the north Norfolk coast which I had first visited with Stan Witcher, to cover again the ground where we had walked together. I began to meet some of the country characters who told me stories of their villages. Many of them have become my friends and have taken me into their homes and lives.

At Blakeney I met John Wallace, who was the uncrowned king of Blakeney creek. I remember him as a short tubby man who, winter and summer, wore his grey flannel trousers rolled up to his calves. On his feet he had canvas shoes with the toes cut out to let the muddy water of the creek flow in and out. Exposure to the winds and sun gave his a permanent suntan. His balding head had a fringe of white hair, which made him look like a monk.

Over the years he put stones and bricks along the creeks making a pathway down to a rickety old bridge which fishermen used to cross the creek. Near the end of the creek there were some sheets of rotting corrugated iron nailed to a wooden frame. They provided a very crude protection from the worst of the winds. Here John and his friends sheltered and it was known to all as 'John's office'.

An old bridge at Blakeney

One day I received a letter from the British Consul's office in Tel Aviv, asking for a painting of Blakeney creek, looking towards the watch house, including the loo and John's office. The official has the painting hanging in his office and in times of stress he says he looks at it and is calmed by the tranquil scene and the peaceful memories which it engenders.

There is a tale about the loo. Apparently a Blakeney man was in it when a German aeroplane crashed nearby, having been brought down by anti-aircraft guns at Weybourne. The pilot and navigator surrendered to the man in the loo, who brought them back to Blakeney and became an instant village hero.

Many times I have walked these creeks, talked to John, and painted them. There is quietness that is broken only by the intrusion of an occasional low flying aeroplane. Otherwise, there is just the call of sea birds — gulls, oyster catchers and wigeon, and the gentle slap of the water as it ebbs and flows in the creeks.

The area had all the elements of the Norfolk coast which I found so attractive. There were the muddy creeks, the dull grey-greens of plants growing in the saltings, boats of all shapes and sizes, either riding at anchor or tilting at a crazy angle in the mud, and over all, the magnificent expanse of the sky.

I began to explore other villages which have provided me with an unending supply of subjects. I visited Wiverton, Cley with its mill, Glandford with its shell museum, Morston and many others. Of them all, I think perhaps my favourite is still Morston. Even to this day it remains largely undeveloped as it is not so accessible as most of the other villages. There are wide expanses of lonely marsh, cut up by innumerable creeks. Some are narrow enough to jump over, others can only be crossed by flimsy bridges.

There was one particular bridge which I often used. It was made of bits and pieces of wood driven into the marsh and rickety planks with slats nailed across them. There was an insecure hand rail, held together by string which gave way if leaned on. When crossing, the planks seemed to dip in the middle before rising to the far bank. It always reminded me of pictures of bridges over jungle rivers, where to cross was to take one's life into one's own hands. This bridge has been altered now and while it may be safer to cross, it has lost much of its earlier character.

As a result of a request from the RNLI at Lowestoft, I have been fortunate in getting to know crews from some of the other Norfolk stations. The painting which I donated for fund raising was to depict the Frederick Edward Crick, which had been on station since 1963 and was nearing the regulation retirement age. It was to show the boat coming into Lowestoft harbour in rough weather. Under such conditions the harbour entrance can be distinctly difficult and hazardous to navigate.

Walls on each side of the entrance restrict the width and cause water to rush and swirl as waves, blown by the wind, break on the jetties. Walls of water charge from one side to the other, throwing boats off course and bringing them perilously near to disaster sometimes. To make sure that I would get the

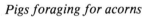
Pigs foraging for acorns

Fishing smack entering
Lowestoft harbour

detail of the hull, superstructure and rigging correct, I spent some time sketching her, lying near the yacht club. Then, with the help of a local newspaper, I found some very good photographs showing lifeboats and ships entering harbour in all sorts of weather. After observing the same scene for myself, whenever I could get into Lowestoft, I was able to create a picture of the moment the lifeboat entered harbour.

During a fund-raising evening at Gunton Hall, the picture was auctioned and the purchaser presented it to the crew to be hung in the clubhouse. Shortly after this, the boat was taken out of commission.

When Tommy Knott, coxswain of the Lowestoft lifeboat retired, he was presented by Lord Somerleyton, President of the Branch, with two of my paintings. Tommy, who won many awards with the RNLI, was described as an outstanding coxswain. He surprised us by choosing two paintings of horses working in the fields, rather than of the sea. He told me this was because they were part of the life he had known as a boy, working with his father on a farm, while he was a part-time seaman.

Later, I met Henry 'Joyful' West and the Sheringham crew. This arose in a curious way as a result of buying a fisherman's smock from a ship's chandler in one of the back streets of Sheringham. As I entered the shop my attention was taken by models in bottles displayed on the shelves, which one of the

West family had made. This had always been an interest of mine and I was determined to meet the maker whom I could see from his work was a real craftsman.

I went to his cottage, quite close to Sheringham front, and was shown in along a passage cluttered with paraphernalia of fishing – cork floats, nets, lobster and crab pots and such like. He showed me some of his models which were very fine, with beautiful detail. The ships were modelled as if at sea, with a slightly forward rake of the mast, on which the carefully fashioned sails were displayed in full. Such was the detail that each ship had a port and starboard light. He demonstrated to me how he sat whittling away to shape the hull and how, piece by piece, he added the rigging and sails.

Subsequently, he made a ship to fit into a three-sided whisky bottle for me. It remains one of my treasured possessions. Typical of many craftsmen, he charged me a ridiculously low price for it. He was obviously spending his time on this hobby because he loved it and had little thought of making money from so doing.

After I was demobbed I spent a week on the Norfolk Broads in a sailing cruiser, little knowing at that time that I would return again and again. In my canoe I have spent many happy hours on the quiet waters of the Bure, away from disturbance from holiday cruisers and other craft. The Broads have always fascinated me and I visit them throughout the year to see the effects of the changing seasons on the trees, plants and bird life. The overhanging willows and the reed beds are particular favourites. I often use a scene from the Broads when I am giving a demonstration. A BBC Radio Norfolk producer was in the audience one evening, when she thought of inviting me on to her programme.

The idea was simple. As I travelled down from Wroxham to Ranworth, I would describe why the Broads were of such absorbing interest to me and, at the same time, I would paint a picture and discuss it as it developed. Also on board would be a naturalist, who was to describe the wildlife around us on various stretches of the river and Broads. In between the talking, records were to be played and the whole programme was scheduled to last two hours.

When I arrived at the mooring near Wroxham Hotel, at the arranged time, all the radio crew were already there but I soon sensed a high tension among them. I politely asked what was happening and was told that the signal obtained from the transmitter on the boat was not strong enough when it had been tested going down the river. I was told that this demanded a change of plan and then came the bombshell – 'We will not be able to leave this mooring'.

To make the programme possible, cables to a mobile trans-mitter on shore had been connected to microphones on the boat. There was no time for argument as the time soon arrived when I heard the presenter saying 'This afternoon we have on board our cruiser at Wroxham, Norfolk, artist Jason Partner, who is well-known for his water-colours of the Broads and North Norfolk coast. As we move down the river, he will describe his feelings for the Broads and why he so often comes here to paint. In the next two hours he is going to paint a typical Broadland scene and will describe how it progresses from blank paper to a complete picture during the afternoon. Over to you Jason'.

I was sitting in the well of the boat, from where I could see about 20 of the radio crew falling over themselves for'ard as they went about their various tasks. There was a massive clock for all to see, but really to ensure that the presenter could keep to his tight time schedule. Looking out I could see some boat sheds painted green, flecks of rainbow colours from some oily water, a scraggy tree, three ancient tame mallards, an odd sparrow or two, an occasional seagull, and a continuous stream of traffic over Wroxham bridge.

Fortunately I knew this stretch of the Bure so well that I could paint a word picture from memory. For the painting I had already done a preliminary sketch from which I worked. Every ten minutes or so I was on the air, talking about the stage it had reached. About halfway through the programme a cruiser came up behind us, wanting to moor there. The radio engineers frantically gesticulated and waved their arms, as they were afraid the boat would foul our cables. They indicated as best they could for the stranger to back off. The man at the tiller shouted to his wife, who was in the bow, to tell her to jump ashore and moor. He obviously had no idea that a radio programme was being broadcast. Having secured his craft, he came over and indicated that he thought he had a perfect right to moor there and told us so in no uncertain terms.

On another occasion I was invited by a BBC television producer to do a programme of painting in Norfolk. The idea was to show how I worked, both out of doors and in the studio. I suggested that the location work could be done at a little village, Burgh-next-Aylsham. Some years earlier I had found a spot where I had since often painted. From my chosen viewpoint I could look across a small river valley, with grassy meadows, reed lined ditches and, on the far side, a thatched church and cottages.

One day, when I was busily working there, the farmer who had given me permission to go over his fields came along. During our conversation he said, 'I suppose you know what this this place is called'.

I had to confess that I was new to the area and had no idea. 'Oh well, it's called Crome's Hole' he said. He went on to explain that John Crome and other members of the Norwich School of Art often came there to paint. They arrived by pony and trap and stayed in the village pub which is still there but it is now a residential cottage. I was thrilled to think that I was in the very area where such great artists had painted in the past.

'The crew were drinking my coffee'

This, then, was my choice for the television programme. I enthused about the beauty of the spot, the perfection of the composition and contrasting shades of colour. I felt that the producer was not very impressed. The problem was that the sun was in the wrong direction for the cameras and it was not possible to 'shoot' the film just there.

A little further along was a lane, or loke, as it was known locally. This was chosen as a suitable spot, and to some extent I was pleased as the hedges provided some protection from the bitter easterly wind that was blowing. It was known locally as a lazy wind, as it was too tired to go round but just 'blew right thro' you'.

The scene that I painted at this new location was across a valley, but this time there were farm buildings with red tiled roofs. In the foreground were meadows, some ivy covered trees and willows which were just acquiring the first faint tinge of spring colour.

After the producer was satisfied that he had all the close-up shots he required, he said the crew would go back up the lane to get a distant shot of me painting. 'Whatever you do, don't look round' he said. 'We don't want to see you smiling into the camera.' I painted on for what seemed ages thinking that at any moment I would hear the command 'Cut' but I heard nothing. In the end, in desperation, I did turn round to discover that the filming had long since ceased.

I learned later that one of the crew had gone to get more film from a van parked near my bungalow. Jo saw him and offered

Climbing the fence at St. Benets' Abbey

to make some flasks of coffee, which she laced with rum because the weather was so cold. By the time I turned round all the coffee had been consumed and none had been left for me!

The film was completed back in the studio, showing me putting finishing touches to the painting. How we managed it I do not know. My studio is really quite small yet somehow the camera crew with their reflection boards, sound men with their 'sausages' and I, all managed to get in.

For another programme I was asked to spend a day with a presenter, who would try to paint alongside me and I would give him help and tuition. This time I chose to go to St. Benet's Abbey, a much-painted scene on the Norfolk Broads.

As we walked along the rough track leading to the ruins, I talked about their history and why they attracted me as they had so many famous artists in the past. To protect the ruins from cattle which graze the marshes, a strong fence has been put round it. The producer suggested that I should be seen carrying my equipment in my canvas bag, climb over the fence and take my bag which the producer would hand over to me. Unfortunately, he dropped some of the things and there was a loud cry of 'Cut'.

Then it was suggested that he should go over first and I would hand the bag over to him. The presenter was wearing a smart pale grey suit and suede shoes, having refused my offer of wellingtons before leaving the car. He climbed over successfully, but as I handed the kit over he stepped back and put a foot into a cow pat. It slipped from under him and he fell into a mixture of well trodden earth and cow dung, leaving his suit badly stained down the left side.

As I was wiping him with handfuls of grass, I was reminded of Alf doing the same for me when I fell into the pig manure.

By this time the producer was getting a little fragile and my suggestion that we should abandon filming and return another day did little to help. 'The film crew has been booked for the day and there is no way I can afford not to complete the assignment today' the producer said in exasperation.

The schedule for filming had to be adjusted to make sure that nobody saw the stained suit. Instead of sitting on a stool the presenter had to sit on a plastic bag which I was able to provide. As he sat uncomfortably on the ground, I explained how to sketch the scene and then paint it, doing a picture myself while he did his best to follow my instructions.

Towards the end of the afternoon, as the light began to fade, reflector boards had to be used in profusion as the camera could only be moved to a limited extent to avoid exposing the offending stains. Eventually, as we went back to the cars, the presenter said he had to get back to the studio quickly as he was reading the news that evening. 'No doubt you have a change of clothes with you' I suggested. 'Usually I carry a spare suit with me but today just when I need it, I haven't brought one' came the reply.

At that time the news readers sat behind a desk, and when he appeared all looked normal, but as I sat and watched I thought 'Underneath that desk is a suit badly stained with cow dung and mud'.

Winter in a Norfolk lane near Foulsham

CHAPTER 9

Selling Overseas

Following one of my early exhibitions there was a favourable comment about my work in *The Arts Review.* This magazine was respected by art dealers, both at home and abroad. Many overseas buyers used it as a guide to contemporary art and for planning their visits to major exhibitions in this country.

A South African was the first visitor to arrive in this way. He came to my exhibition, liked what he saw, and asked if he could be an agent for me in his country. We arranged for the despatch of some pictures for sale in his Johannesburg gallery. They sold well and he asked for more. This arrangement lasted for a few years, after which he moved to another part of South Africa and I lost contact with him.

My contacts in Canada were established through a client and friend in this country. This client's daughter, Mrs. Carol Brenan, worked hard to promote my work there.

When Jo and I visited Canada at the invitation of the Brenan family, we stayed with them in a charming old colonial style house at Rothsay, New Brunswick. This is a part of Nova Scotia which strongly reminded me of my commando training days in Scotland. With its hills and numerous creeks and inlets, it is easy to see why emigrants from the Old World moved to this province from the land they had left behind. Some of the wide rivers were being used to float huge rafts of timber from the forests down to the saw mills. They could only be crossed by ferries, but across some of the narrower rivers there were a few remaining covered bridges. The sloping roof was designed to protect the bridge from accumulating heavy falls of snow which would block it, and by the weight might even destroy it. Many have been pulled down but now a society has been formed to protect these unique pieces of Canadian history.

Across the rivers, nestling on the hillsides, were villages with small white churches particularly noticeable. They had towers which made them look like Swiss churches in the Alps.

Mr. Brenan senior took us to his 'Point house' on the edge of one of the inlets. Outwardly, it was in the style of an early frontier cabin, built entirely of timber. Inside it had every modern facility, although Mr. Brenan had, as far as possible, used beautifully restored furniture of the early settler period. We slept in wooden bunks and ate very large steaks barbecued on the veranda.

He showed us around the area in his huge Cadillac, of which he was justifiably proud. We went to William's lake and while we stood beside it I enquired how it got its name, 'Well, I guess' said he in his Canadian drawl, 'a guy called William must have found it'. Beaver were at work making a lodge, the maples were a riot of colour, from brilliant scarlet to bright yellows. Small farms, with patches of green pasture, dotted the hillside. The whole scene might well have come straight out of Hiawatha. The diversity of colours, combined with the clarity of light, made this an artist's paradise. I spent every spare moment working with my pencil and brush.

We went through vast areas of woodland where abundant wild life could be seen. Here porcupines, moose and bear roamed. Mr. Brenan warned us about the moose, which might suddenly appear on a track. Standing seven to eight feet high, with antlers spanning anything from six to eight feet, they looked ferocious and can be very dangerous, especially when they have a small calf at foot.

There was an additional danger from the moose hunters, many of whom came from America with a permit to kill a certain number of birds and animals. I was warned that whenever I went into the woods during the hunting season I must wear the brilliant fluorescent red jacket with which I was provided. This amused me as it was in complete contrast with the dull green clothes I was accustomed to wear when with a shooting party. It was soon explained to me that with the hunter's motto 'If it moves, shoot it and answer questions later' accidents can easily — and often do — happen.

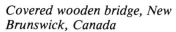

Covered wooden bridge, New Brunswick, Canada

I think Mr. Brenan felt that I was particularly vulnerable as if I was sitting in the undergrowth, I might easily be mistaken for an animal. For safety I was advised to whistle all the time, for 'nobody has every shot a whistling moose'.

In the rivers I saw brown bears catching salmon in their paws. Sometimes the old bears were accompanied by a cub, which would eat the fish while it was still held by the older animal. Also on the water were blue winged and green teal, and black ducks. Overhead, one occasionally heard the sound of geese migrating south as this part of Canada is on one of the flight lines. The Indians used decoys to bring some of the birds down, and then shot them with bows and arrows.

When a consignment of my paintings was received, the Brenans held a drinks party, displaying and selling them in their home. While Jo and I were visiting them, they held one of these parties and during the evening I found myself talking to the producer of a local television show and somewhat unwittingly, agreed to appear on her programme.

On the appointed day, a car was sent to take me to the studio which was housed in a vast high-rise building. I took little notice of what was happening as I was taken, by lift, up several floors to the hospitality room, to meet the presenter. Here I was offered a drink of anything I fancied to steady my nerves and we had a short chat before I was taken to the sound room for voice tests and thence to the make-up room.

Finally, I was taken to the studio and the show began with me explaining why I was in Canada and how I painted my pictures. Then, quite unexpectedly, I was asked if I could show some of my pictures and the equipment I used. Everything had been left in the car so it was agreed that I would fetch them and rejoin the show a little later on.

Unfortunately, I was left to find my own way down to the car park and back. After asking the way, I eventually found the car and was on my way back when I realised that I did not know which floor the particular studio was on. Having found the right floor, I then had difficulty in finding the correct room. I found myself listening at doors as I had terrible visions of entering the wrong studio, appearing like a lost soul in the middle of a serious economic discussion programme, or worse still, a drama production, dodging in and out of the scenery trying not to be seen while making my escape. I chuckled to myself thinking of these possibilities, as I crept from door to door, listening at each one, and I visualised somebody suddenly appearing in the corridor and wondered what they would make of this peculiar behaviour.

Eventually I found the right door and entered, to be amazed at the apparent total disorganisation behind the scenes, while in front of the camera everything was running so smoothly.

While visiting Europe to purchase paintings for sale and for clients, Mr. William Ash, owner of the English Gallery, Boston, Mass., called to see my work. He purchased a few water-colours and after they had been sold, he asked for some more.

In the second year he decided to put on a one-man exhibition and invited me to open it and talk to his clients. It was arranged that Jo and I would spend a few days in Canada, after which she would return home, while I would go on to Boston.

The gallery owner had made a great effort to make the show a success by inviting a large number of guests, and informing the local television and radio networks, both of which were to be present to interview me. The plan was for me to arrive a few hours before the official opening.

I flew into Logan airport, excited at the prospect of seeing my paintings hung in a gallery new to me, and in meeting people who were obviously interested in art and to find out how they reacted to my work.

When passing through customs I was taken to one side by a uniformed young lady and told to 'Hold it right there' while she made a telephone call. I was soon aware that three uniformed police were drifting towards me and I was invited to 'Step to one side'. By this time I was getting a little concerned and explained why I was in Boston and that I was being met at the airport.

'What is the problem, and will it take long?' I ventured to ask. 'Just come over here, we want to talk to you' came the reply. It was then explained that the visa which I had obtained through a travel agent was valid in Canada but not in America.

Stretham steam pump, Old West River, Cambridgeshire

Then I was taken into an office where the scene reminded me of an episode from 'Kojak'. There was one policeman sitting at a desk facing me, and two at the back, one of whom was continually moving to one side. Each had a gun under the flap of his jacket, and each had a very short 'crew cut' hair style. They reminded me of scenes so frequently seen on television.

They then proceded to give me a third degree interrogation, firing questions so quickly that before I had time to answer one, another had been asked. 'What are you doing here? How long do you intend to stay? Where have you come from? How are you going to pay for your hotel? Are you aware that the USA is being continuously infiltrated across its borders by illegal immigrants? Do you intend to live on the USA social system as a bum?'

I explained again the purpose of my visit, told them the name of the person who was waiting for me and gave them the address I had just left in Canada but they seemed not to take any real notice of my answers, being more intent to keep up the harrassment by their quickfire questions.

I managed to ask how, arriving at Logan airport could be compared with attempting to slip across the border, but I could see that such remarks were not being very well received and fell silent for a time.

They assured me that I was in deep trouble and I asked if I could speak to the British Consul but was told that this was not possible at that moment. Then I asked if I was being accused of anything and if I was, what could I do. I was also getting very anxious about the gallery owner who was, as far as I was aware, still waiting for me, without having been told of the reason for my delay. They refused to put out a call for him so that he could come forward and verify my position.

At this stage I was allowed to call the British Consul but he was away and there was nobody there to help me. Then the policeman at the desk pushed a form towards me and said 'Sign this'. I said that I was not in the habit of signing forms without reading and understanding them and asked for an explanation of what it was about. 'If you sign it, it will indicate that you do not wish to stay in the USA'.

To this I replied that judging from the welcome I was getting, I was not keen on staying for long. This remark upset them again and I was told that they were tired of people like me − bums and bankrupts − trying to sneak in and get a living there without proper work permits.

I realised that the discussion was getting me nowhere and sought to establish what rights, if any, I had to appeal against being held in this way. The options were not very great. I could, if I wished, go into the 'downtown jail'. This was a very old building, and had I accepted, I would have been, in all probability, put into a cell occupied by a motley crowd held under suspicion of offences ranging from petty crime, to mugging, drug running or murder. There I might be held for

two to three weeks until the circuit judge arrived to hear my case. I asked, as a matter of interest, what the conditions were like in there and was promptly told 'You mustn't think we're going to put you in the Hilton Hotel and pay for all your board and lodging'.

The other option was to be deported to my country of origin. I said that I had arrived in Canada but came from England. 'In that case, we'll send you back there' I was told.

In the meantime, they had condescended to find the gallery owner, who was brought up to the office and he was allowed to take me, on 1,000 dollars bail, to the exhibition for four hours. He whisked me into his car and drove like a demon to the gallery to get me there for the official opening. For the next two hours or so I mingled with the visitors and talked as best I could, keeping an eye on the clock all the time.

When the time came, I was spirited away to Logan airport where I found the immigration authorities waiting for me. Two FBI agents in plain clothes promptly snapped handcuffs on me and I was taken down through various lifts and back passages on to the airport to the waiting 'plane. Imagine how I felt as I was marched across the tarmac and up the steps. At the top I was handed over to the stewardess who had to sign for me. Just before take-off the handcuffs were removed and the FBI agents left. I felt that everyone in the 'plane was staring at me, wondering what sort of criminal I was, being deported from America.

When I arrived, I rang Jo who said 'You sound remarkably clear' to which I replied 'I should be, I'm at Heathrow'. She was astonished as she had been expecting a call from Boston.

I was very annoyed at the whole affair as it had cost a great deal of money, taken up many days of planning and travelling and achieved very little. I visited the American Embassy in London and was told how concerned they were by illegal immigrants crossing both the Canadian and Mexican borders and the determination of the authorities to stamp it out. In the end, the spokeman was very apologetic and issued me with a visa which enabled me to take any member of my family into the country, for an unlimited stay, over a period of ten years.

CHAPTER 10

Commissions

Over the years, undertaking comissions for my work has occupied some of my time. They can be very rewarding, both from a financial and artistic point of view, but they can also be challenging and especially if the scene which I have been asked to paint does not provide a satisfactory subject.

The commissions which fill me with the greatest apprehension are those where the prospective buyer gives an enthusiastic description of a favourite village, building or of his or her home. Beauty is in the eye of the beholder and what seems to be a wonderful subject for a potential client, does not always inspire me. Nevertheless, I try hard to do as I am asked, even if this does mean that a favourite old shed or fence or tree, which really spoils the composition of the picture, has to be included. For such commissions, artistic licence will only stretch as far as leaving out television aerials and electricity poles.

Some of the most challenging are those which start with a telephone call requesting a painting of – say – a Broadland scene for a retiring colleague. It is explained that he or she is an admirer of my work and has specified that a painting by me would be most gratefully received. This usually takes about ten minutes to explain. Then I ask 'When do you want it'.

This is followed by a slight pause, then 'Er, well, she is, er, leaving next week'. This means that I have seven to ten days (or even less) in which to do the painting, get it mounted, framed and perhaps delivered. Nevertheless I value this type of work as I often know, or know of, the person involved and feel that it is a further extension of the close relationship with my clients which I value so highly.

Commissions can arise in all sorts of ways. Some years ago now, I donated six small paintings to be auctioned to raise funds for the RNLI. At the auction was Jimmy Evans, who was so impressed with them that he wanted to see more and, as far as I am aware, he now has the largest collection of my work. Through him I met one of his friends who particularly wanted a picture of Lincoln Cathedral.

It so happened that the view he wanted was from the south side and the very best place to sit was in the central reservation of a busy dual carriageway. Early one Sunday morning, when the traffic was light, I took my stool and settled down for the morning. As the day progressed there was a steady build-up of traffic, some of which seemed to slow down as a curious driver tried to see what an idiot artist was doing sitting in such a spot. I became terrified in case a driver should be distracted by me and cause an accident. By midday there was so much traffic that I was nearly choked by the exhaust fumes which accumulated between the two lines of traffic. Later, this painting was donated to the City of Lincoln Museum.

Jimmy also introduced me to another friend, Sir Richard Wakeford, who invited me to stay in a lodge on Speyside so that I could paint views of the river and of the salmon fishers. The banks at this spot are unusually steep for a game fishing river, which necessitates using a rather special cast to avoid fouling the banks or overhanging trees. The art is to make sure that the line is above the head and is then cast forward towards the salmon as they come upstream.

I spent many happy days beside the Spey, watching the ghillies or water gamekeepers taking fishing parties along the various beats. They walked in the river, wearing chest waders and feeling for large boulders or deep water with a long thumb stick. This was a marvellous area for painting with the light greens of the broad leaf trees standing out amongst the dark pines which covered large areas of the banks. Then there was the constant bubbling of water as it poured over the rock strewn river, eddying round the larger boulders where the river was shallow.

Fishing on the River Spey

A few years ago I was asked by the chairman of the Lincolnshire Agricultural Society to paint a picture of the village of Falkingham, where the society — one of the oldest in the country — was founded.

The village has some tastefully restored old houses and buildings, opening out on to a square. Among them is a beautiful old coaching inn, where the Society was formed. The picture, which was to be of this view, had been sponsored by a bank for presentation at the Lincolnshire Show that May.

In early spring I commenced working on it, positioning myself down a slight hill, looking up towards the square. I made an early start and picked the spot from which to work. About an hour later, when I was making good progress with the sketch, a huge van housing the mobile library pulled across on to the green, completely obscuring my vision. It stayed there for about an hour and a half, while a steady stream of villagers clutching small piles of books, emerged from nearby cottages.

Two days later I was nearing completion of the picture when another huge van parked in exactly the same position. This time it was the mobile bank.

While I was waiting for it to move I had a walk round the village and was most interested in the 'correction' house. This dates from early Victorian days, when local villains were sen-

Shrimp boats at King's Lynn

tenced to work for a period on the treadmill, which was contained within. The last man to work it was sentenced to one month on the treadmill for stealing some hay. The dungeons were also still there.

The picture was duly completed and presented to the chairman who then asked me to paint the village from the opposite direction, and this I managed to do without further problems from parked vehicles.

One of the commissions which gave me most pleasure to undertake was a view of Walberswick for presentation to Charles Rounce when he retired as Manager of the Assembly Rooms in Norwich. Much of the success of the exhibitions I held there in those days was due to his encouragement, help and understanding. I am delighted to think that of all the numerous artists who exhibited there while he was manager, he chose a painting of mine as his retirement gift.

Even after a lifetime of painting, I still get tremendous satisfaction from going out with my pencil and paints. Whenever I am walking in the countryside there is always an exciting possibility that a view will provide a new subject to paint. It still gives me a thrill when I get out my sketch book or water-colour board and start to work.

Art has given my life fulfilment, I had to struggle in the early years to achieve my lifelong ambition to be an artist and to take on Dan's cloak. But it was all worthwhile and I have tried faithfully to follow his example, and the traditions of the Old English School. I hope that this account of my life will give the reader some idea of the enjoyment that painting has given me.